Winner's Guide to

NINTENDO®
GAME BOY™

Winner's Guide to

NINTENDO®
GAME BOY™

Kate Barnes

HAYDEN BOOKS

A Division of Howard W. Sams & Company
11711 North College, Suite 141, Carmel, IN 46032 USA

International Standard Book Number: 0-672-48490-0
Library of Congress Catalog Card Number: 90-61221

Acquisitions Editor: *Marie Butler-Knight*
Manuscript Editor: *Joe Kraynak*
Production Coordinator: *Becky Imel*
Illustrator: *T.R. Emrick and Don Clemons*
Designer: *Glenn Santner*
Cover Artist: *Eric Lindley, Partners, Inc.*
Production Assistance: *Brad Chinn, Sally Copenhaver,
Denny Hager, Tami Hughes, Bill Hurley,
Chuck Hutchinson, Jodi Jensen, Lori Lyons,
Jennifer Matthews, Joe Ramon, Dennis Sheehan,
Bruce Steed, Mary Beth Wakefield*

Printed in the United States of America

Contents

Introduction, *vii*

Acknowledgments, *ix*

Game Boy Games

Alleyway, *1*
Baseball, *6*
Boomer's Adventure in ASMIK World, *12*
Boxxle, *26*
Flipull, *32*
Golf, *39*
Hyper Load Runner, *48*
Kwirk, *53*
Malibu Beach Volleyball, *63*
Motocross Maniacs, *68*
Nemesis, *73*
NFL Football, *79*
Revenge of the 'Gator, *86*
SolarStriker, *93*
Space Invaders, *99*
Super Mario Land, *104*
Tennis, *111*
Tetris, *116*
The Bugs Bunny Crazy Castle, *122*
The Castlevania Adventure, *128*
Quarth, *135*

Introduction

Nintendo's Game Boy offers something for everyone. Pack along a Game Boy, and you can take along freakish escapades, intriguing mind benders, competitive sports, fantasy filled outer space adventure, and games with a cute twist just for fun. You'll find low levels of play for beginners as well as higher levels that are sure to stump the most savvy of gamesters.

As you're packing, don't forget your *Winner's Guide to Nintendo Game Boy*. This book reveals tricks, tips, and new ways to approach each game. By following the hints and strategies included in this book, you'll get more satisfaction in less time. Of course, many of the Game Boy games are so complex, that even a book ten times this size couldn't cover the games step-by-step. So, what you'll learn inside are the best strategies and the *most useful* tips.

If you rent or borrow the Game Boy games and don't get the manuals that come with them, use the "Let's Play" section of each chapter to get the basics. After you get the basics down pat, move on to more advanced play.

Because different players approach games differently, two imaginary game characters talk about their approaches. Throughout the book, you'll hear strategies from Hi and Tec, a dynamic duo who don't always agree. You'll see that Hi and Tec focus on different aspects of the games, giving you two unique perspectives.

I hope the techniques in this book help improve your play. If you discover strategies or tips of your own, send them to me in care of the publisher. If I use your pointers in the next edition, I'll mention your name.

Enjoy!

Caring for Your Game Boy

Treat your Game Boy right. The following rules and precautions will make your Game Boy last and will help you get the most out of your game play:

- Make sure your Game Boy is OFF every time you swap cartridges. Otherwise, your cartridge is going to wear out long before it's due.

- Always insert the cartridge with the label out.

- Remember, scores and other information specific to a particular game are kept in memory which is erased when you turn off your Game Boy.

- Keep fresh batteries in your Game Boy or use . the special rechargeable battery pack specially designed for Game Boy.

- Don't forget to take breaks. That little screen can make your eyes mighty tired after an hour of play.

- Finally, be aware that taking the Game Boy to school or work can be disastrous, unless you exercise extreme control in keeping your hands off the little doohickey.

Some Game Boy games are great for a two-player rivalry. You'll need two Game Boys and a copy of the same game cartridge in each one. With both Game Boys OFF, connect them with the Video Link cable. Then, power up and be ready to beat the pants off your pal!

Acknowledgments

Thanks to Jeff Cochran, Bill Drouidllard, Sharkie Khorsandi, Jeff Perry, and Julia Wesley for their assistance in game play.

Trademarks

All terms mentioned in this book that are known to be trademarks or service marks are listed below. In addition, terms suspected of being trademarks or service marks have been appropriately capitalized. Howard W. Sams & Company cannot attest to the accuracy of this information. Use of a term in this book should not be regarded as affecting the validity of any trademark or service mark.

Alleyway™, Game Boy™, SolarStriker™, Super Mario Land™, Video Link™, and Nintendo® (Nintendo of America Inc.)

Boomer's Adventure in ASMIK™ World (Asmik Corporation of America)

Bugs Bunny™, Honey Bunny™, Sylvester™, Wiley Coyote™, Daffy Duck™, and Yosemite Sam™ (Warner Brothers)

Boxxle™ (Fujisankei Communications International, Inc.)

Castlevania—The Adventure™ and Konami® (Konami Industry Co., Ltd.)

Flipull and Space Invaders (Taito America Corporation)

Kwirk™ (Acclaim Entertainment, Inc.)

Hyper Load Runner™ (Bandai America, Inc.)

Malibu Beach Volleyball™ (Activision)

Motocross Maniacs™ and Ultra® (Ultra Software Corporation)

Nemesis™ (Crystalline Creations, Inc.)

NFL™, team names® and team logos® (National Football League)

Revenge of the 'Gator™ (HAL AMERICA, Inc.)

Tetris (V/O Electronorgtechnica)

Alleyway

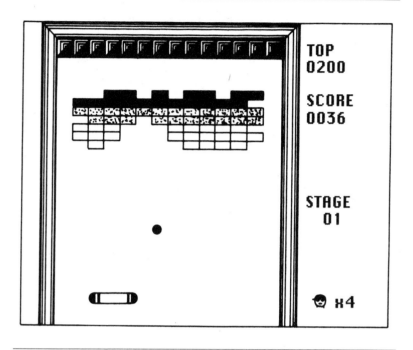

TOP
0200

SCORE
0036

STAGE
01

🙂 ×4

Description

You're trapped! The only way out is to break through the walls ahead of you, and there are many of them. Your way out? Four powerballs. Use your paddle to whack the balls against the bricks and blast your way through. The further you go and the more points you rack up, the larger the number of balls you have remaining. Clear all 32 stages and be ready for the fanfare!

1

Let's Play

Keep an eye on the screen to see your score, the top score, and the current stage (up to 32). Use the following buttons to control your paddle:

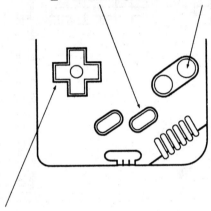

■ Start game.

■ Pause the game.　　Release the ball.

■ Move paddle left or right.

■ Press with button A to speed up paddle.

■ Press with button B to slow down paddle.

Strategies

Hi's Hints

Start with your paddle in the center of the screen. After you hit the ball, bring the paddle back to the center. By keeping your paddle in the center, you're in a better position to hit the ball when it bounces back.

Use one finger (try your thumb) to move your paddle—you'll be able to move a lot more quickly than if you keep switching fingers.

Try to see in your mind how the ball is going to bounce back. Imagine a real ball hitting a wall at the same angle. Where will it go after it hits the wall? Well, that's a pretty good indication of how the "ball" will bounce on screen. Pay attention to the angle at which the ball goes toward the wall. It'll bounce back at the same angle.

You can use the paddle to redirect or put English on the ball. In other words, you can make the ball spin so that it takes some funky bounces. For example, if you hit the ball off the end of your paddle, you can change the angle of the ball. The ball will run across the screen rather than bouncing up to the ceiling. If you move the paddle in the direction that the ball is coming from, you'll send the ball back in the same direction. This is called "slicing the ball." Slicing has the added advantage of slowing the ball down.

The game offers up to 32 stages. Each stage has different characteristics. For example, the first stage is very simple; you have to make it through a wall with two gaps on either side. The fifth stage is a little more difficult. The wall consists of a checker pattern with some missing bricks. The ball may bounce several times before coming back down.

The wall in each stage consists of three layers of bricks: white, gray, and black. Each white brick is worth 1 point, gray bricks are worth 2, and black are worth 3 points. Be careful when you hit grey or black bricks—the ball bounces back mighty fast. Use your powers of imagination to guess where the ball will bounce, and then get your paddle over there . . . pronto!

Tec's Tips

Within each stage, you'll encounter the following 4 game patterns:

1. Normal screen.
2. Scrolling screen.
3. Advancing screen.
4. Bonus screen.

Normal—The normal screens are easy to dispose of—they don't move. When you have a gap on the side (as in Stage 1) try to hit the ball into the gap. The ball will bounce off the ceiling then back to the top layer of bricks several times, destroying a lot of bricks. Have your paddle ready when the ball comes back down. Warning: Watch out when you're in Stage 4 or above—when you hit the ceiling, your paddle shrinks!

Scrolling—On this screen, the bricks move from right to left. As they disappear from the left, they reappear on the right. This makes it more difficult to get the ball to break through the walls or fit in the gap . . . if there is one. With a little patience and a quick paddle, you can do it. The good news is that the scrolling screen actually makes it easier to hit individual bricks that are left toward the end of the stage (for example, when you have only 3 bricks left on the screen).

Advancing—The advancing screen is much like the normal screen except that every so often the bricks move down the screen toward you. What makes this particularly nasty is that when the ball bounces off the advanced bricks, it has a shorter distance to travel. In other words, it comes back a lot faster. Especially difficult are the higher stages. Once the bricks advance beyond a certain point, they disappear. You won't have to worry about them, but you won't get points for them either. When the bricks get close to you, try to avoid them. Go for the higher bricks—you'll have more time to hit the returning ball.

Bonus—The bonus screen appears at the end of each stage. Instead of bouncing off the bricks, the ball wipes them out. The object is to nail as many bricks as possible. Get 'em all, and you get an added bonus. Whatever you do, don't send the ball back in the same direction it came from—it'll just pass through empty space. Try hitting the ball on the end of the paddle to make it go across the screen. This takes a little more time, but you have a better chance of bagging the remaining bricks.

Finally, I want to say a few words about the A and B buttons. Don't bother with them until you feel comfortable with the game. When you get to later stages (such as the Stage 10 advancing screen), you'll see that you can't move the paddle fast enough. At this point, use the A button to speed up your paddle and the B button to slow it down. You can also try the A and B buttons to aim the ball when just a few bricks are left or when you're on a bonus screen.

Other Pointers

- On the bonus screens, you can knock out a bunch of bricks early—just move slightly away from the direction in which the ball is coming.

- In Stage 7, hit the ball on the end of the paddle to make it go across. If the ball gets trapped in the middle of the bricks, you'll hit a bundle of them!

- In Stage 10 and up you'll find unbreakable blocks on the screen. Use them to bounce the ball back and forth to zap the other bricks.

Manufacturer Information

Company: Nintendo of America Inc.
Address: P.O. Box 957
        Redmond, Washington
        98073-0957
Game Play Counselors: 206-885-7529 (This is a
        regular toll charge telephone call.)
Typical Price: $19.99

Baseball

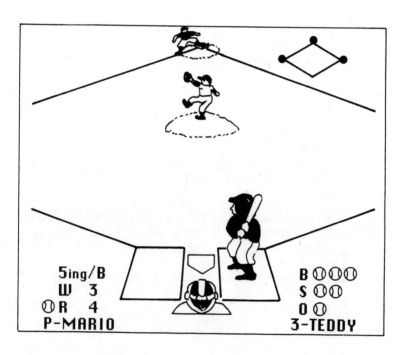

Description

Game Boy Baseball puts America's favorite pastime right in the palm of your hand. The White Bears, with their power hitters and some of the best base runners in the league, square off against the Red Eagles, who have the best left-handed pitching staff east of the ol' Mississippi. Knock the dirt off your cleats, step up to the plate, and come out swingin'!

Let's Play

Whether you're throwing a fastball or trying to hit one out to the bleachers, you'll need to use the following controls:

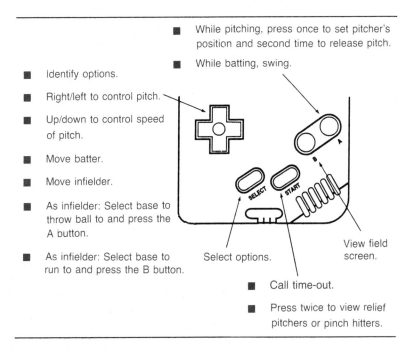

■ While pitching, press once to set pitcher's position and second time to release pitch.

■ While batting, swing.

■ Identify options.

■ Right/left to control pitch.

■ Up/down to control speed of pitch.

■ Move batter.

■ Move infielder.

■ As infielder: Select base to throw ball to and press the A button.

■ As infielder: Select base to run to and press the B button.

Select options.

View field screen.

■ Call time-out.

■ Press twice to view relief pitchers or pinch hitters.

Before you start, choose your mode: USA or Japan. Each offers different teams and unique players. Choose to play with one or two players, select your team and your starting pitcher, and get ready. Just like real baseball, you play nine innings to determine the winner. There's even a built-in slaughter rule—get 10 runs before your opponent scores, and you win!

Strategies

Coach Hi's Hints

To start with, study your opponent, find out the strengths and weaknesses of each player on the opposing team. Know the strengths and weaknesses of each of your players, as well. Remember, you're not only a player, but a manager, too.

Before you choose which batter to send to the plate, look at the available information. You'll learn the player's batting average, whether he's left- or right-handed, his batting ability, and his skill or bunting ability. For example, Eddie has poor batting ability but a good skill rating. In other words, he's good at bunting, but if he tries to hit the long ball, he'll probably go down swinging. If you want to keep the opponent guessing, let Eddie come out swinging, but don't get your hopes up.

Each pitcher has his own strengths and weaknesses as well, so check out who's pitching before you decide how to swing. For example, if you're facing Luigi (a good fastball pitcher), press the A button to swing quickly. Randy (with his sharp curve balls) requires a slightly slower swing. Be careful, though, these guys will surprise you.

Watch where the pitcher is standing, and adjust your position. For example, if the pitcher is standing to the far right and you have a left-handed batter, move toward the plate a little. Otherwise, he'll kill you with pitches to the outside. You can also move closer to or farther from the pitcher to control the height of the ball after you hit it. For example, if you move toward the pitcher, the ball goes higher. If you're trying to hit a homer, this is a good move, but more often than not, you'll hit a pop-up. Welcome to the big leagues!

Want to bunt? Tap the A button. To hit to right field, hold down the A button for a second. Hold it down longer to hit to middle or left field.

If you're in a forced-run situation, keep an eye on your runners. When the pitcher hurls the pitch, the runners usually start running automatically to the next base. Sometimes though, you might have to start them out; press the base direction where you want the runner to go and press the B button. But be careful! These pitchers don't like to give up stolen bases.

If you have a guy on first and you hit a single, you can advance the runner on first to third. No big deal, right? If you're fast though, you can usually stretch your single into a double; the third baseman is no golden glove—you can beat his throw. If you start to run toward second and you don't think you'll make it, press the first base button and button A at the same time to run back. Do this even if it looks like the second baseman will be able to throw you out at first. You can usually make it back safely. Be cautious about sliding, though. When you get close to a base, you can't return.

Coach Tec's Tips

Since Hi covered batting pretty well, I'll act as your pitching and fielding coach. First of all, pick a pitcher with some stamina so you can stay with him for a while. Otherwise, he'll get tired and start slowing down—they'll hit everything he pitches. If you want to pick a pitcher with lower stamina but a good fastball (like Luigi), then keep an eye on the radar. When you see his pitches slowing down, it's time to go to the bull pen and get a fresh pitcher on the mound. Don't wait till some slugger takes ol' Luigi's pitches downtown.

9

Know the batters. If you're pitching to Eddie, who's no Babe Ruth, don't waste your time. Give him three fastballs down the ol' gullet, and he's outta there! On the other hand, if you're pitching to John, who can hit any pitch within a mile of the plate, mix your pitches. Throw a curve ball or two. Lob a change-up over the plate. A lot of batters can't handle outside pitches, but they'll go for a fastball no matter where it is. So what? Try throwing some fastballs outside by pressing the left or right arrow after the pitch. They'll go fishing, and you can chalk up some strikeouts.

No matter how good you get, the batters are going to connect with a few of your pitches. If you happen to be unlucky enough to give up a home run, you can't do much but watch it fly over the outfield wall. If somebody hits the ball to the outfield, don't worry too much. Outfielders are pretty much automatic in their game—you usually don't need to do anything. The outfielder will automatically position himself to get it. But if the ball travels deep to center field, you might have to move your center fielder up or down to catch the ball. If runners are on base, throw the ball as soon as you catch it to get them out or keep them from advancing.

You have a lot more control over the infield. When the batter hits a grounder or a line drive, be on your toes. Move your closest infielder in the direction of the ball, and scoop it up. Catch it in midair, and the batter's out. If it's a grounder, throw it to one of the bases to nail an advancing runner or throw it to first to get the batter. Play smart and be quick—you might be able to chalk up a few double plays . . . triple plays?

When a fly ball is hit, the runners may take off before the ball is caught. Remember, they must tag up after the ball is caught, or they can't advance. As soon as you catch the fly, throw the ball to the base where the runner started. If you're quick, your opponents now have two outs!

If you're playing the infield, you can get a runner out in any of three ways—throw him out, tag the base he's running to, or tag him with the ball. To throw a runner out, point your fielder to a particular base and hit the A button to throw the ball. If you're close to the base, get the ball, and press button B to run to the base. To tag a runner out, get the ball, and press the arrow key to move toward the runner.

If your infielders miss a ball and it rolls to the outfield, run the outfielder to the ball. He will automatically pick it up. Point him to a base and hit the A button. Outfielders can't run with the ball—they have to throw it.

Other Pointers

- Study your opponent!

- Although it helps to have quick reflexes, playing smart is more important. Know what kind of pitch to throw each hitter and know each opposing pitcher's weakness. You'll do a lot better playing intelligently than if you try to strong-arm your way to the pennant.

- When you're out in the field, think about where you want to throw the ball *before* the batter hits it. If there's a guy on first, look for the double play.

- You can't steal a base until the pitcher starts his windup.

Manufacturer Information

Company: Nintendo of America Inc.
Address: P.O. Box 957
         Redmond, Washington
         98073-0957

Game Play Counselors: 206-885-7529 (This is a
regular toll charge telephone call.)
Typical Price: $19.99

Boomer's Adventure in ASMIK World

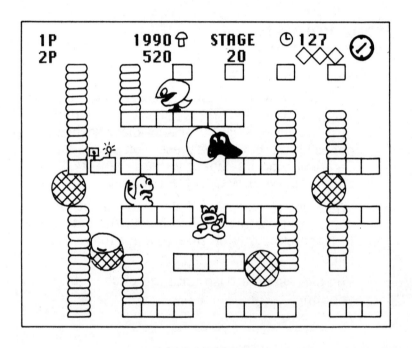

Description

Little Boomer needs to climb to the top of a tower. Sound easy? Well, there's a little more to it. You see, Boomer isn't going to the top of the tower to view some pretty scenery. Boomer's going there to meet with and destroy the evil Zoozoon, the Lord of Darkness. And if that's not hard enough, Boomer has to fight back down to ground level after completing this quest!

Let's Play

Use the following buttons to move Boomer from place to place and to use the special items:

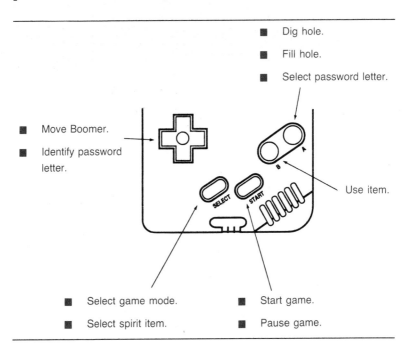

■ Dig hole.

■ Fill hole.

■ Select password letter.

■ Move Boomer.

■ Identify password letter.

■ Use item.

■ Select game mode.

■ Select spirit item.

■ Start game.

■ Pause game.

13

Before you begin, you can choose to start a new game (1 or 2 players) or enter a password (provided by the game) to continue an old game.

Boomer's adventure takes him through 8 Worlds, with 8 Stages in each. That's 64 stages, folks. Worlds 1 through 4 get Boomer to the top of the tower (and to the dreaded Zoozoon). Worlds 5 through 8 return him to the ground.

Each stage has a hidden key to unlock the door to the next stage. Be quick—time is important. Any time remaining after you unlock the door to the next stage gets added to your score. To keep the bad guys away, you can dig or fill holes. If a nasty guy is chasing you, dig a hole. When the guy falls in the hole, Boomer can cross it. Fill the hole in (with button A), and the guy's buried—he will bother you no more. The only rule is that you can't dig a hole on top of another hole or too close to the wall.

At the top of the screen, you can see the stage number and the number of Boomers left (there's a whole family of them). The time left along with the item for Boomer to use is also shown. What items? You can find and use the following items that are hidden around the screen:

Time bomb—to get a bad guy or dig 5 holes at the same time (use the B button).

Shovel—to dig a hole quickly (use the A button).

Snow cone—to freeze the bad dude (use the B button).

Chili pie—to breath fire (use the B button).

Boomerang—to destroy the enemy (use the B button).

Bone—to disable or smash the bad guy ONCE (use the B button).

Compass—to point Boomer toward the key, up to FOUR times (use the B button).

Detector—to beep as Boomer gets closer to the key (use the A button).

Roller skates—to move quickly (use the A button).

Ski boots—to slow down (use the A button).

Spirit—to switch to any item (press Select until the item appears then press the A or B button).

Egg—to get an extra Boomer.

Strategies

Hi's Hints

This is a fun game—you can learn a lot just by playing around with Boomer. For example, I found that I could rotate Boomer without moving him by just pressing the A button and turning in the direction I want to go. When you first start out, play around with Boomer till you feel pretty comfortable with the controls.

If you want to get very far in this game, you'd better learn to dig and fill in holes. When you dig holes, always finish your digging. If you don't, the holes will only slow down your enemies—shallow holes will not trap the enemy, which is what you want to do. You don't want to have to deal with this guy again, do you?

Go for items that will help you move up and down the tower. These items are not all that easy to get a hold of, however. Some characters will tease you with certain items. They'll hold the item just long enough for you to dig your hole. Then, just before you can trap them, they'll bury the item so you can't get it! You have to be quick. In the Boss stages, you can dig up only a certain number of items. In some stages, a character will dig up the key and bury it somewhere else before you can get to it.

The trick, of course, is to figure out the location of the key in each level and survive long enough to find it and get to an exit. If you know where a key is, don't head right toward it. The enemy will surround you and finish you off before you can use it. Work your way around and back to the key.

Once you get the key and head for the exit, you aren't home yet. Watch out for enemy characters lurking in the exit. They're just waiting for you to try that key.

You'll meet bad guys galore in this game. Here are a few tips to help defeat the nasties:

Bouncer—Find the roller skates first then hit Bouncer with bones. The shovel is a big help . . . if you can find it in time.

Moth—Moth can only be hit when he's near the ground and not firing at you.

Spike—Continue moving from corner to corner and use the bones or the boomerang to defeat Spike.

Beetle—Beetle shoots a deadly thread toward the blocks—steer clear of them.

Zoozoon—Roller skates and the shovel are a must. Find a boomerang and wait at the bottom of the screen. As soon as you see Zoozoon, throw the boomerang. Just before he moves, hit him again.

Tec's Tips

I'm no locksmith, but I know where to find keys, at least on the way back down. The best hint I can give you is that the keys are in the same place going down the tower as they are going up. When you kill Zoozoon in Stage 33, turn around and go down the tower the same way you came up. The only difference is that the entrances and exits are reversed.

The diagrams below show you where to find keys. The maps also show you where to look for goodies. Good luck—the maps show you where to look, but with a bunch of enemies chasing you, it's not as easy as it looks!

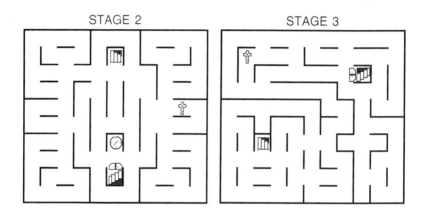

STAGE 2   STAGE 3

STAGE 4

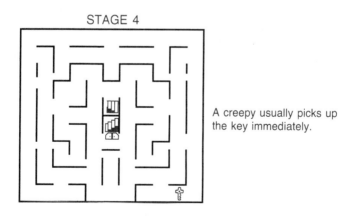

A creepy usually picks up the key immediately.

STAGE 5   STAGE 6

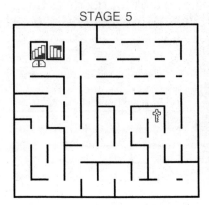
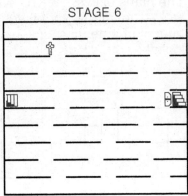

STAGE 7

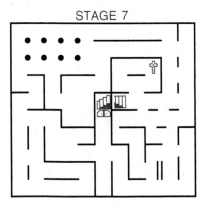

STAGE 8

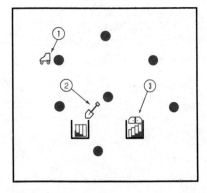

EXAMPLE

Password:
AXOLOTL

1. Go straight to this point to dig up roller skate.

2. Run here to dig up shovel.

3. Run around and dig up bones to throw at boss.

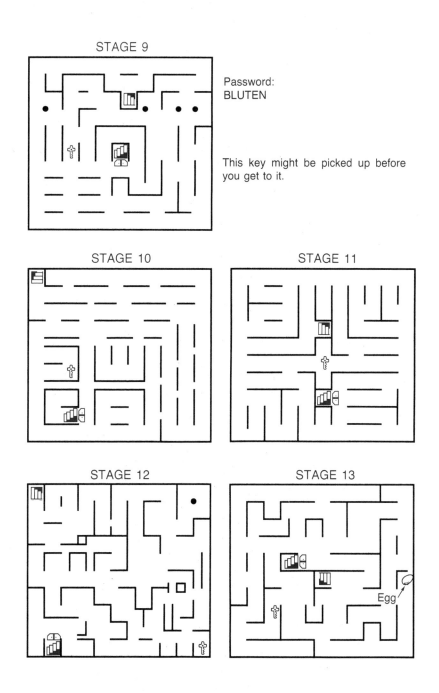

STAGE 9

Password:
BLUTEN

This key might be picked up before you get to it.

STAGE 10

STAGE 11

STAGE 12

STAGE 13

Egg

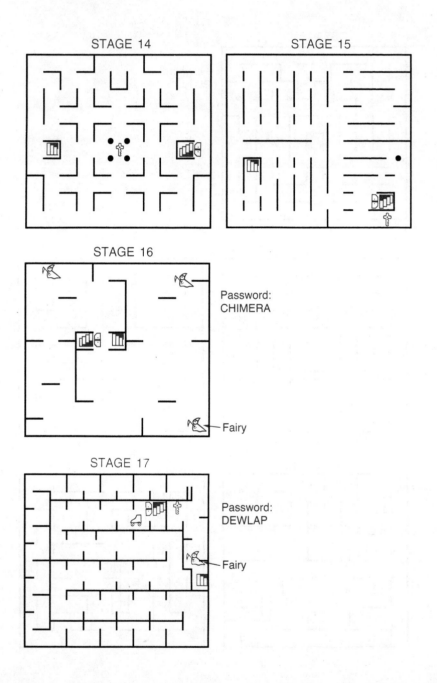

STAGE 14

STAGE 15

STAGE 16

Password:
CHIMERA

Fairy

STAGE 17

Password:
DEWLAP

Fairy

STAGE 18

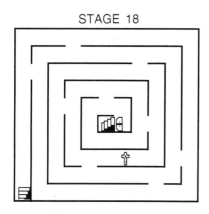

STAGE 19

Shovel

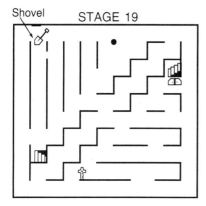

Watch out! If you dug a trap or hole for these guys to fall in, they like to bury the items they have before you can trap them.

STAGE 20

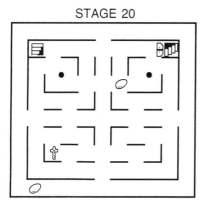

STAGE 21

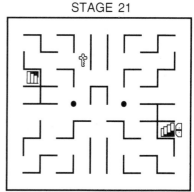

STAGE 22

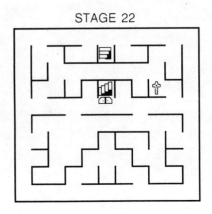

STAGE 23

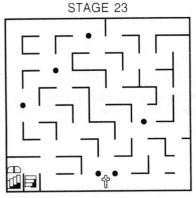

Password:
ELYTRON

Watch out for creatures. They'll appear as you go for the stairs.

STAGE 24

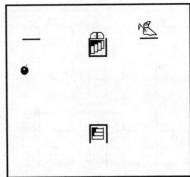

Password:
GILA

If you leave too many items on the screen, no more will come up.

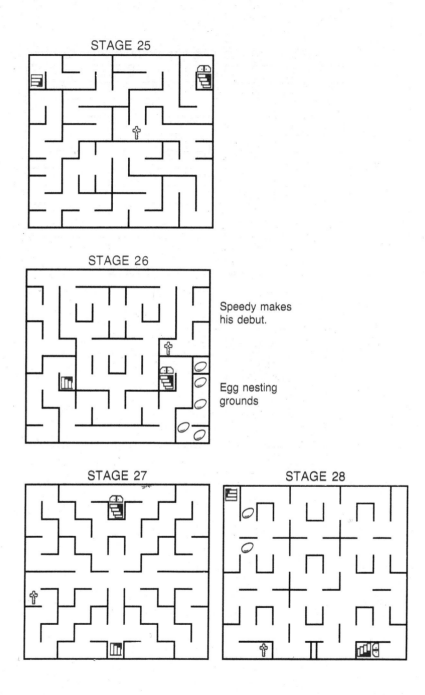

STAGE 25

STAGE 26

Speedy makes
his debut.

Egg nesting
grounds

STAGE 27

STAGE 28

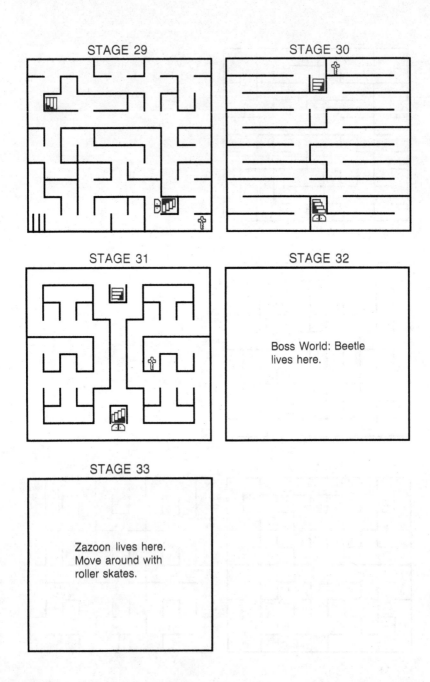

STAGE 29

STAGE 30

STAGE 31

STAGE 32

Boss World: Beetle
lives here.

STAGE 33

Zazoon lives here.
Move around with
roller skates.

Other Pointers

- In the Boss stages, the roller skates and the shovel are a great help.
- Here are the passwords to get you into advanced stages:

Stage 8	AXOLOTL
Stage 9	BLUTEN
Stage 16	CHIMERA
Stage 17	DEWLAP
Stage 24	ELYTRON
Stage 25	GILA
Stage 32	HYDRA
Stage 33	IBEX
Top of the tower	JEDOCH

Manufacturer Information

Company: Asmik Corporation of America
Address: 444 South Flower
Suite 1600
Los Angeles, CA
90071-2975
Telephone: 213-624-5104 (This is a regular toll charge telephone call.)
Typical Price: $19.99

Boxxle

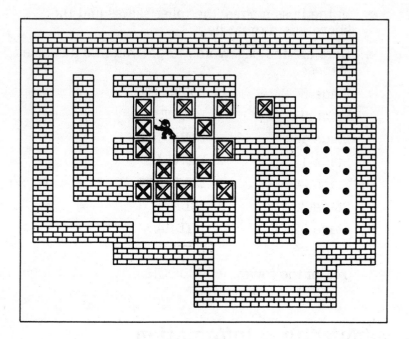

Description

To start out, let's introduce the main character—we'll call him Willy. Willy works in a warehouse, moving boxes and crates from one location to another. For Willy to do his job right, he has to move each box and crate to its dotted destination. Sound simple? Well, a few of the boxes slip into place pretty easy, but very few. You'll need to plan ahead, learn simple strategies, and then huff and puff. Although *Boxxle* seems like a simple game, it demands foresight, planning, and strategy. What do you get when you win? The age old prize: the girl. (Nobody said this game was set in the 90s)

Let's Play

Use the following controls to shuffle those boxes around:

- Identify menu options.
- Move character.

- Select item on menu.
- Back up one move.

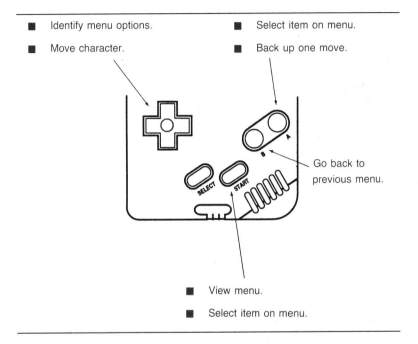

Go back to
previous menu.

- View menu.
- Select item on menu.

In *Boxxle*, you may solve existing warehouse puzzles or create your own warehouse riddle. When you select Play to solve the existing puzzle, you're given two options:

- *Play*—to begin at the beginning.

- *Passkey*—to continue an earlier game with the passkey given. (Press B to erase an incorrect passkey letter, then press End and A to complete the passkey entry.)

Each warehouse area consists of ten screens. Pick the one you want to tackle by pressing the Select button. If you muff a screen, press Start then select Retry.

Look in the upper right corner of the warehouse floor screen. You'll see the area and screen number followed by the number of moves made on that screen.

Strategies

Hi's Hints

One of the most frustrating parts of this game is getting your box stuck against a wall. So, don't push a box against a wall unless you're *absolutely sure* that's what you want to do. If you do happen to get stuck, however, there's some good news—if you touch the little arrow keys, you can move the man and the box one step at a time. You're never stuck between the columns. When you think you're stuck, don't try to force it with big, long runs. Easy does it. Tap, tap, tap that controller, one step at a time, till you're free.

Although you can usually free yourself when you get boxed in, don't count on it, especially when you're moving near the outside wall of the maze. If you push a box up against the outside wall of the warehouse, you won't have many choices as to where to move next. Even the tap-tap-tap technique won't get you out. You might need to consider starting the level over.

If you're having trouble figuring out how to move a box to the target dot, think back to the earlier, easier screens. The pattern you used to move a box to a similar location earlier will probably work just as well on this screen.

The screens with the little boxes on them are tricky. My advice is to hold the game up close to your face. After a while, you'll see those boxes just as well as the other ones.

Plan ahead. In other words, before you do anything, figure out what you're going to do. In the early screens, you don't have to plan very far in advance—you can take a box from where it is, move it all the way through the screen, and set it right onto a dot. As you progress, however, it gets a little more tricky. You need to think about moving several boxes, a little at a time, so they'll all eventually find a place. In other words, if you move one into position too early, you'll block the others.

Remember that when you get two boxes side by side, touching each other in any direction, you cannot push along that direction any more. If you put boxes too close to one another, you may just get boxed in. Therefore, keep the boxes from touching each other while you're still arranging them.

Look at the boxes. Sometimes, the boxes themselves will become part of the maze, helping you figure out an effective strategy.

When you first start on a screen, be patient. Don't start moving blocks around without thinking. Your first moves may well determine the outcome of the game. If you start out in a position that makes you feel trapped, look at which boxes and which moves will give you more options in the future. Then, make those moves. After making a couple of good moves, you might begin to see more possibilities, and the game may start to open up. In general, put boxes near the place they'll end up, but out of the way.

Tec's Tips

I really don't get too worried about the number of moves I make on a screen. What I really want to do is move the boxes where they belong and get on to the next screen. Only a very advanced player should be interested in finding out the absolute minimum number of moves necessary to complete the screen. If you're a beginner, just worry about solving the puzzle. After you beat the game a few times, you can start working on bettering your score.

For most of the screens, there's only one solution that makes sense. Once you figure it out, it's pretty hard to cut down on the number of moves.

Don't automatically assume that a box belongs on the nearest dot. It's usually better to go for the most difficult dot first. Look for the dot that's closest to the wall or near some hard-to-move objects, then go for it. If you can get a box on top of the hardest dot, the rest of the screen is a piece of cake. This strategy has an additional pay-off: Since the hardest dots are usually in the most out-of-the-way places, you're probably not going to need to push any other boxes through there later. If you go for the easier dots first, you'll end up blocking access to the more difficult ones.

Just because a box starts off on a particular dot doesn't mean that the box has to stay there. Keep your options open. Frequently, a box that's sitting on a dot at the beginning of the round is going to be in your way the whole time. If it'll open up the screen for you, move the box. You can use the block to finish off the puzzle later. Quite often, in fact, the end of a level consists of several little moves—bump, drive around somewhere else, bump, move Willy, and bump—to move the boxes to their final positions.

Keep a little pad of paper nearby to write down the pass keys that you've saved from the areas. There are ten screens in each area. The Select option only lets you work among those ten screens. To get to a screen in another area, you have to use your pass key, so keep track of the pass keys for each area.

If you're wondering how to get into a new area in general, here's the secret. Go into the last screen in each level, and win that screen. Each time you successfully complete a screen, you get a Next feature. Use this feature to earn your way into the next area. In other words, instead of working your way through all ten screens, you defeat only the last screen in each area to get the password. Pretty soon, all of the screens are available for you to choose from.

If you use the "build your own warehouse" option, you're in for a special treat. This will take a lot of trial and error, but it's a good exercise for your mind. Make a screen that's challenging, but not impossible. You don't want every player in the household collapsing from frustration, do you? This will give you a real appreciation for the designers and programmers that built the 108 screens in the game.

Other Pointers

■ If you get frustrated on a screen, use the Select option to move on and play one of the other 108 screens.

■ You can use the password feature to save the game up to the point you're at.

■ The game offers a backup feature that lets you go back and correct a move, but you can correct only the move you just made.

Manufacturer Information

Company: Fujisankei Communications International, Inc.
Address: 150 E. 52nd Street
New York, NY
10022
Game Hotline: 708-968-0425 (This is a regular toll charge telephone call.) 8 a.m. to 7 p.m. Central Standard Time
Typical Price: $24.99

Flipull

Description

At first, it looks like a simple game—you throw a block that has a certain symbol on it and try to knock down other blocks that have the same symbol. Yes, it *sounds* simple enough. But when you start playing, the strategy gets increasingly interesting and the time increasingly tight. You'll need to stay several steps ahead of the game. Plan your moves, anticipate the moves of the game, and you just might have a chance. Think strategically. Always anticipate. Learn to predict. Then, make your move.

Let's Play

The screen has a pile of blocks, you're holding a block, and there's a blob (yes, a blob) on screen that you have to move around; the blob throws your blocks for you. The goal is to remove the necessary number of blocks from the screen in the allotted time. Each block has one of the following five symbols:

- ⊙   Circle Block
- ⊠   "X" Block
- ☐   Square Block
- T   Taito Block
- S   Special Block

The following buttons put you in control of the game:

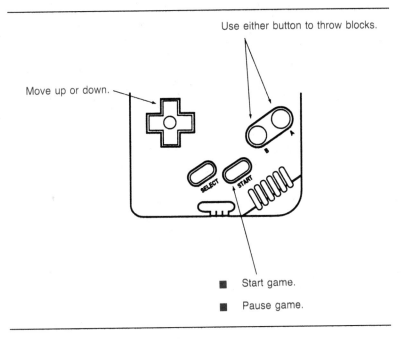

Use either button to throw blocks.

Move up or down.

■ Start game.

■ Pause game.

You need to hit the blocks that have the same symbol as the block you (or your blob) is holding. You can earn a special block by hitting five blocks in a row with a single block. Earn one of these special blocks, and you can use it to hit any block, no matter what symbol it has.

Use the ceiling if you like to bank your shot into the pile. Keep an eye on the right side of the screen; it provides the following information:

Clear—indicates the number of blocks that make up a clear screen. If only this number of blocks remains on screen, you may continue to the next stage.

Time—shows the interval you have remaining before time runs out and you lose the stage.

Block—indicates the number of blocks you have remaining in the pile. The Block number minus the Clear number equals the number of blocks you have to remove in the Time remaining. Actually, if you have the time, the game lets you go farther for more points before you get stuck. Then, the game declares Clear! and stops the play.

Stage—shows you the level of play you are in and identifies the number of special blocks you have remaining. (You receive special blocks in each stage.)

At the top of the screen is your score. The Scoring goes like this:

Number of Blocks Cleared	Points Awarded
1	100
2	400
3	900
4	1600
5	3200

If you clear all blocks and have time left, each second left is multiplied by 10 points, and that's added to your score. You also get 1000 points for winning the game plus 1000 points for each additional block you hit. The game is over when time runs out or when you get a block you can't play.

When you bomb out of a stage, the number of credits is displayed. You start with three credits and lose one each time you fail to complete a stage successfully. Lose your last credit and you have to start all over at Stage 1. *Flipull* has fifty stages, so you have some work (and some fun) cut out for you.

Here are some special pointers for the two-player game. If you manage to clear multiple blocks, your partner gets them. That's no way to make friends, but it's a great way to win. If either of you clears five blocks in a row, a special block shows up in the pile, and you can both go for it. If your friend is getting a little too far ahead, try this: Pile your pal's stack of blocks to the ceiling. That'll keep her busy!

Strategies

Hi's Hints

A great way to learn some strategies is to watch the self-running demonstration at the beginning of the game. Just leave the machine running on the main title screen. Eventually the demo will start. It demonstrates Stage 1. You can see the strategy and even memorize it by looking for the pattern of play. There's a pattern for every stage of play. Hi and I have had our own matches to see who can get through Stage 1 faster.

Don't waste any time at the start. As soon as you press Start, the clock starts running. As soon as the game takes you to a new stage, the clock starts running. Figure out your plan of attack, and get to it!

You'll often start out with the special block. When you do, quickly scan the pile to see if you can hit more than one block. If you can nail a bunch of blocks, you'll rack up some big points early.

When you see the word "Miss!," you'll typically get a special block. Be ready for it.

The next block you'll get to throw has the same symbol as the block immediately past the one you hit, so make sure you can use this block for your next throw. For example, if the pile has no blocks with squares and you hit a block with a square block behind it, you get a square block, but you can't use it. The message "Sorry No Next Move" will appear on screen, and you will have lost the round.

Once in a while, you'll see the words "Hurry Up!" go across your screen. As these words go across, both the play and the score freeze. You can do one of two things: You can get aggravated, because you already know you're in trouble; or you can use the time to ignore the words and study the pile or check your score. Use the time to plan your strategy.

Plan every move. If you accidently shoot your block at a block with a different symbol, you lose time. Not only do you lose the time it takes the block to go and come back, but you also lose time while you watch your blob wiggle nervously. You can't fire right away, and you waste precious seconds. In other words, think before you shoot.

When you lose the final game allowed, the game stops and you have to start again at Stage 1. Yes, that's right, you have to do the same old screens over again, just to get to an interesting level. Boring, to say the least. If you want to make this process a little more challenging, start the game by setting a goal, such as "no errors until Stage X." To play error free, try to memorize the patterns at each level. That way, you can breeze through the lower stages. Also, you'll be less likely to make foolish mistakes at the lower stages and lose valuable credits that you'll want to blow later, in tougher stages.

Tec's Tips

The lower stages give you enough time to play pretty successfully without tons of planning. As you get into higher levels, you need to plan more. You'll see pipes that you can use to deflect your block, and you'll see more opportunities to use blocks that seem unusable. Just about all the bad things that can happen to you at lower stages are compounded at the higher stages.

At the higher stages, keep sizing up the pile as you go. Try to develop the habit of keeping one eye on the clock and the other on the number of blocks to go. This will motivate you to work faster. Hi thinks this is a waste of time. She'd rather just work as fast as possible and let the blocks and time take care of themselves. Do what works best for you.

Hi already mentioned that you should keep an eye on the block that's past the one you're trying to hit. My tip is to think even further ahead. When you throw your block, you'll have a pretty good idea of which block you're going to get next, so start thinking about where you're going to throw it. As you fire one block, think of where you're going to throw the next one.

If you do get the message "Sorry No Next Move," you can press the Start button. The game you got hung up on will be over and you can continue that stage to try again. Your credits are also shown. This shows you how many more games you can lose before you are bombed out of the stages and have to start over at Stage 1, drats!

At first, it's difficult to see how to hit the blocks at the top. An arrow appears to identify which block you'll hit if you throw your block. As long as there are no pipes to deflect off of, when you move up the arrow moves right and when you move down the arrow moves left. The arrow shows the final effect of bouncing off the top of the screen. If the block can ricochet off pipes, the movement of the arrow is a little more unpredictable. Believe the arrow; it is one hundred percent accurate.

Once in a while, you'll think that you should be able to hit the pile from the top, but the angles and pipes just won't let you do it. Again, believe the arrow.

As you get more experienced hitting the pile from the top, try to get a feel for what kind of hits are possible. Looking for the arrow is helpful, but it takes precious seconds off your clock. If you can get a feel for it, you'll save yourself some time and probably some credits.

If you have a choice of hitting two different blocks with the same symbol in different spots in the pile, go for the one that will give you the best advantage. What's the best advantage? Well, that depends. If you can hit more than one block at a time, go for it! Unless, of course, that will leave you with a useless block. Wiping out a series of blocks with the same symbol will give you big points. Also look at the backup blocks to see which block you'll get for the next throw. Try to get a block that will let you hit a series. Always, avoid getting a block that you can't use for your next throw. Try wiping out a block to create a string of blocks with the same symbol. That way, you might be able to nail a string of blocks on one of your next throws.

Other Pointers

- You can press the Start button to pause at any time. When you do, the pile is no longer displayed, so you don't really get an opportunity to size up the stack. This does give you a break, if you're getting tired, and that may be just what you need.

- Always take a tiny bit of time to examine the pile, especially when you get a special block. You may just find a spot where you can hit a string of blocks.

- When you shoot into a row that has two blocks alike separated by a blank space, your block will travel right through the blank space and nail both blocks at once.

- Keep tapping the arrow keypad while you move. A lot of the moves cover just a few spaces, and tapping gets you there with accuracy. When you want to make a longer, faster move, practice holding down the button. But watch out. You run the risk of overshooting and then having to tap, tap, tap to get back.

- As you get in higher stages, you can't throw a block through the side of a pipe; however, a block can pass through the top of a pipe.

- Even after you've cleared the number of blocks
  required, keep going for points (1000 for each
  block you clear past the required number).

Manufacturer Information

Company: Taito
Address: 267 West Esplanade
  North Vancouver, B.C., Canada
  V7M 1A5
Technical Support: 604-984-3040 (This is a regular
  toll charge telephone call.)
Typical Price: $24.95

Golf

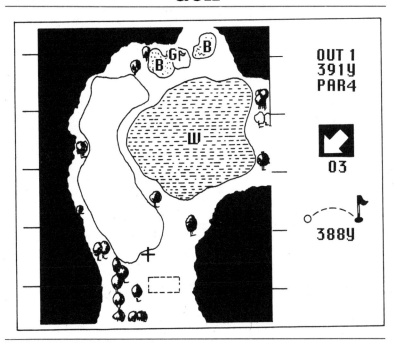

Description

There's nothing like golf on a breezy spring day. You stand at the tee and see hundreds of yards of perfectly manicured green carpet stretch out from beneath your feet. The wind moves through the trees and sifts through your hair. Sounds almost relaxing, except for the fact that you're playing golf, one of the most frustrating games on the planet. Getting a one and a half inch ball into a four inch hole sounds easy enough, but when you try it, it's enough to make you forget the beauty of it all!

Let's Play

Use the following buttons to take your shots and control the screens:

- From the Play screen—up/down to select clubs, left/right to control direction of shot.

- From the Hole or Green screen—scroll the screen.

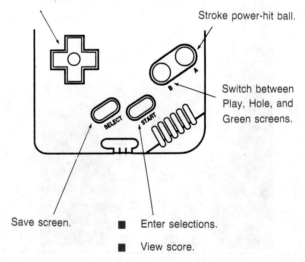

Stroke power-hit ball.

Switch between Play, Hole, and Green screens.

Save screen.

- Enter selections.

- View score.

At the start, use the A button to enter your name on the Name Registration screen. (Use the B button to delete a letter if necessary.) On the Course Selection screen, select Japan or USA, then press Start. On the Game selection screen, identify which game to continue, or choose to start a new game and press Start. On the Player Mode screen, select Continue to continue a saved game, New Game to begin a new game, or Best Score to see the scorecard of the best game for each course. As you play, you'll see the following three screens:

Play—The shot direction indicator appears. At the bottom of the screen, you'll see the following information:

■ The number of strokes you've taken.

■ The number over or under par so far.

■ The distance the ball is from the hole.

■ The club selected.

■ The status of the ball.

■ The wind condition.

Press the A button to see the player and the shot indicator. Press B to go to the Hole screen.

Hole—You can see the entire hole, including hazards, shot direction indicator, hole number, distance of hole, par, wind, and the distance from the ball to the hole. Press A to go back to the Play screen or B to go to the Green screen.

Green—You can confirm the pin position and see the green detail. Press A or B to go to the Play screen.

To hit a ball off the tee or on the fairway, move the shot indicator with the directional control. From the Play screen, press the up or down arrow to select the club. Finally, press the A button on the Play screen to see the shot indicator. This indicator gives you a picture of your swing.

Press the A button to move the right cursor and take a backswing. (The farther back you go, the more power you can get into your swing.) Press the A button again for the cursor to move left for the downstroke. The farther left the cursor goes, the stronger the swing. Press the A button again to hit the ball. To slice (curve right), stop the cursor to the left of the dark area. To hook (curve left), stop the cursor to the right of the dark area. Usually, you'll want to stop the cursor right in the middle for a nice, straight shot.

You can also control the height of your shot. Press the directional control down while swinging to hit a ball high. Press it up to hit low. Press it left or right in the dark area for backspin. You can get a super shot off the tee by using a 1W (1 wood).

To putt, press the A button to take your backswing, then press A again to hit the ball.

To see your scorecard, press Start while on the Play screen. To reset the game, press A, B, Select, and Start at the same time. To go to training mode (to select any course and hole), hold the directional control down and press Start from the Title screen.

You can save a one-player game, turn off your machine, then return to play again. Here's how: While on the Play screen, press the Select button and follow the prompts.

Two can play this game. Each hole is a match, and the game shows which player is up. A handicap can be set for the less experienced player. Sudden death takes care of any questions of superiority.

Strategies

Hi's Hints

Golf belies any notion you may have that Game Boy offers only less complex, silly games. This one's a real challenge!

Like real golf, the most important thing to learn is how to swing your club. If you don't get almost all of the power on the shot indicator, your ball won't go very far. If you hit outside the straight zone, you'll be all over the course—in the water, the sand, and the rough. If you're interested in sight-seeing, that's great, but it'll destroy your score.

To learn to hit the ball, use the practice option. This won't help you figure out individual holes, but it will help you get your basics down pat. Always anticipate. Rather than look at the spot where you would like to go, look in front of the spot and pick a marker. When the cursor passes that point, hit the button. In the time it takes you to hit the button, you'll end up on target.

The width of the black zone on the shot indicator varies from club to club. It's harder to hit a straight shot with a long club than with a short club. So if you're going for a short shot and you want some accuracy, use a shorter club.

When you've mastered your swing, the next thing to think about is selecting a club. Use the right club for the right shot. Be familiar with the types of clubs and their ranges. The yardages that the machine hits are pretty much the yardages an average golfer (not a pro) would hit. The following yardages are only accurate when there's no wind, when your ball's on the fairway, and when you hit the ball just right.

Keep this table in front of you when you play the game. At first, you'll need to refer to it pretty often, but after some time, you'll get a feel for the clubs, and you can put away the table.

Club		Yardage
1W	(1 wood)	240
3W	(3 wood)	225
4W	(4 wood)	215
1I	(1 iron)	205
3I	(3 iron)	190
4I	(4 iron)	180
5I	(5 iron)	165
6I	(6 iron)	150
7I	(7 iron)	135
8I	(8 iron)	120
9I	(9 iron)	110
PW	(pitching wedge)	90
SW	(sand wedge)	70
PT	(putter)	30

One rule: watch the wind, watch the wind, watch the wind. *Always* check the wind indicator to see how much wind you have. When the wind indicator is a zero or one, it isn't much of a factor. When it gets to be a two or three, you'd better figure it in when you take your swing. When it's four or higher, take it into account when you pick your club. When you're hitting into the wind, it helps to hit a low ball, so the wind can't catch it. To hit a low ball, press the directional control up during the downstroke.

The wind is not always bad. Sometimes when you're in a tough situation, it may even help you get your ball over an obstacle.

Stay on the fairway. Shots from the rough don't go very far. If you need to take a shot out of the rough, choose the next club higher than the one you would use under normal circumstances.

If you're in a bunker, use your sand wedge. The book that comes with the game says that you can use the pitching wedge, but it's difficult to control. The game seems to be a little more generous if you use the sand wedge.

Watch out for the trees. If you get in the trees, it will take you several shots to get out. If there's a tree in front of you, don't assume you'll hit over it . . . no matter how far away it is. If it's far enough away, you will fly over it, but don't count on it. The high ball is the way to get over the trees. To hit a high ball, press the directional control down during the downstroke.

If you're just starting out, don't even try to shoot over a water hazard. Forget par. The water hazards will kill your score. Before you try clearing a water hazard, make sure you can hit the long ball pretty consistently. There are lots of water hazards and they're big (especially on the Japan course).

Tec's Tips

There isn't a big difference between the Japan and USA courses. They both have a lot of water and other hazards. The basic techniques of play apply to both. The only difference is that the USA course is a bit more difficult—the greens are more challenging, and the fairways have a few more slopes and breaks. So, if you're starting out, you might want to try the Japan course first.

Judging how hard to hit putts is one of the most challenging parts of the game. Use the practice option to putt around on the practice green. This will give a feel for the putter and a feel for how the ball breaks on slopes. You'll still have some trouble on individual holes, but you'll putt with a little more confidence.

When you're putting on a level green, the shot indicator should swing in proportion to the length of the putt. If you're putting downhill or uphill make the appropriate adjustments. Be sure to watch the slope of the green, and play the break. Ignore the break, and you'll miss the hole for sure.

When you're on the green, the arrow can be confusing. It's easy to see where you're aiming, but the arrows are set as though you're standing behind your ball looking forward. They're not set according to what you see on your screen.

For a really short putt, don't worry much about lining it up. Just go tap tap with the A button, and the ball will drop right in the hole. No gimmes! The hole's not over till you sink the putt.

The wind can have a strong effect on how close to the flag you can hit. You can adjust your lie to take the wind into account. Another alternative is to slice or hook the ball into the wind to make your shot sail straight and true. This is an advanced move. You have to hit your last touch on the shot indicator early or late to control your hook or slice. Good luck!

The shot indicator is basically a linear scale. That means that the distance the indicator goes is proportional to the distance you're shot goes, assuming you land in the power zone when the shot is over. This is useful to know for judging the lengths of putts, chip shots, and shots between clubs. In some cases, you might want to use a club with a slightly longer range and adjust the end of the distance scale so you don't hit the full shot. Just go for a fraction of the shot you want.

It's important to use both the A and B buttons. The A button gives you control over how you hit the ball, but the B button lets you see the hole so you can line up your shot. Power without accuracy won't do you much good.

The lie indicator shows you where your ball is. When you're in the rough, be sure to check the indicator and choose your club accordingly.

Many beginners forget to change the club after their shot. Don't forget. The club is shown in the lower-right corner of the screen. Just press the directional control down or up to change the club. When you're selecting a club, remember that it's difficult to hit a full shot. You have to get right up to the end of the shot indicator, and that takes timing and practice. If you need distance, consider going up one club.

Take more or less club to stay away from trouble. If all the trouble is behind the hole, take less club or put a little less power into your stroke. If the trouble is in front of the hole, use more club, and try to shoot over the problem.

Other Pointers

- If you're on the fairway or hitting a long approach shot to a hole, be sure to hit the cursor twice. If you hit it only once, you'll be penalized for a miss.

- If you're hitting off the tee and hit the cursor only once, your direction arrow is affected. Reset it to the fairway instead of the flag.

- If you hit the cursor only once on a chip shot, you aren't penalized. This helps you get the exact length you want.

- Check your direction after every shot. Otherwise, you'll always be shooting toward the hole, and that may not be where you want to go.

- You can get a super shot off the tee with a driver—the 1W (1 wood). You can use your driver from the fairway, but don't expect to see the little black bar at the end of the shot indicator. It's gone.

Manufacturer Information

Company: Nintendo of America Inc.
Address: P.O. Box 957
    Redmond, Washington
    98073-0957
Game Play Counselors: 206-885-7529 (This is a
    regular toll charge telephone call.)
Typical Price: $19.99

Hyper Lode Runner

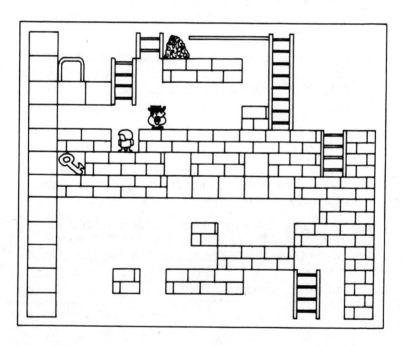

Description

You're the amazing Hyper Load Runner, the famous gold digger from 1849. But, hey, this isn't the 1800s! Somehow, you've gotten stuck in some time warp and have been transported to the future. And you just happen to be smack dab in the middle of a gold mine. What luck! The only problem is that while you're trying to dig, a bunch of robots are chasing you through the mine. Nothing's perfect. If you can get past these guys and ransack the gold mine at the same time, you'll be the richest forty-niner west of the San Andreas Fault!

Let's Play

Use the following controls to move through the mine and dig:

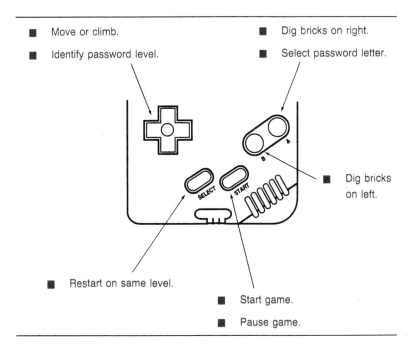

■ Move or climb.

■ Identify password level.

■ Dig bricks on right.

■ Select password letter.

■ Dig bricks on left.

■ Restart on same level.

■ Start game.

■ Pause game.

The game offers several modes of play: Game mode (for one player), Edit (for creating your own screen), and VS (for two players). Start with any one of the first 16 levels. Dig up bricks, collect gold, and use the ladder to escape to the next level.

Strategies

Hi's Hints

The object of the game is to make it through the mine—a challenging maze. In the maze, you can dig up piles of gold to increase your wealth and add to your score. But at the same time, you have to watch out for the bad guys—the little robot-like creatures that chase you around the screen.

How well you can move around the screen depends mainly on how well you can dig. Don't bother trying to look for doors—if you need to get from one area of the mine to another, dig. If you need to get away from some particularly pesky robot, dig a hole and climb through. Be careful, though; you can't just dig any old square. The plain-colored squares won't budge.

Digging does more than just get you through the maze, however. If you need to get rid of some bad guy for awhile, dig a hole in his path. When he falls in the hole, drive over his head, and get on with your business. Of course, this only slows him down. If you want to do away with him for a longer time, you'll have to bury him. Let a bad guy get close, then dig several holes in a row. As you dig the next hole, the previous ones start to fill in automatically. If a robot happens to be in one of the holes at just the right time, he's a goner, at least for awhile. In the higher levels, the guy you bury can drop down on you later from a hole in the ceiling, but at least you had some breathing room.

If those aren't enough reasons to dig, then consider this: Most piles of gold are not just laying out in the open—most of it's buried, and that means (you guessed it!) digging. You'll have to use the beginner or advanced digging approach, depending on the location of the gold.

You don't have to dig for every nugget of gold, however. There are other ways to get it. If you see a pile of gold hanging in midair, go with the rope. Hit the down arrow to fall through space for the gold. You can also get gold by stealing it from a bad guy who picked it up. If the bad guy falls in a hole, the gold goes over the bad guy's head. Drive over and pick up the loot. Finder's keepers . . . .

Be careful when you're digging holes. If you fall in, there's no way to jump or go up. You get trapped, the bricks reappear, and you're dead!

It's possible to dig on the run. Once you clear a spot, just keep digging. Be careful, though. Before you enter a long corridor, make sure you can dig through the floor. Otherwise, you might get into some serious trouble.

Tap and move your way across the screen to dig a long trench. Usually, such a trench will kill any robot that's following you.

Watch out for groups of robots. You can trap the first one in a hole, but the others will drive over their buddy's head and get you.

Don't be too sure you've won a level until you see the ladder that will take you to the next level. If the ladder doesn't appear, that means that at least one of the bad guys has some gold that you need. Dig a hole for this guy, get the gold, and get up that ladder!

The levels in this game are not in order of difficulty. Level 1 is not the easiest. Level 16 is not the hardest. If you're a beginner, find a screen you like between Levels 1 and 16, and use it to practice. You have to work your way above Level 16. (Write down the passwords and use them later).

 Tec's Tips

The best way to clear a screen is to go for the easy stuff first. After you get all that, go after the harder items.

There may be a whole area on the screen in some out-of-the-way place. You may need to move down the ladder and take out several bricks in a row to make a good size hole. Remove the gold, wait for the bricks to reappear, kill the bricks again, and reenter. You may have to reenter the area several times to completely clear the screen. Don't expect the bricks to reappear immediately. It takes awhile.

The screens are often similar. The robots move pretty much the same in any screen. Don't waste your time going over what you already know. Go to an area of the screen that you're unfamiliar with and explore. Who knows, you might learn something!

Occasionally you'll find a pitfall . . . rather suddenly. It looks like a normal brick, but when you step on it, you're in for a ride—down and fast! You may fall through several levels before it's over. Don't worry too much; pitfalls rarely drop you somewhere where you can't get out. You may even be able to use a pitfall to your advantage. For example, you can dig your way down into the level that has the pitfall and pick up a few goodies. When the bricks reappear overhead, trapping you, step on the pitfall for a quick escape.

Beginners will think that robots are bad guys to avoid. That's a pretty good rule, in general, but sometimes you can get the robots to do some of your work for you. Let the robot find the gold. When he's got it, dig a hole, and wait for him to fall in it. When he does, race back and nab the gold. You're home free!

Other Pointers

- There are three ways to get points: gold (150 points), keys (250 points), or clearing a level (500 points).

- The bad news is when you die (after three men) you have to start over again. You get new men when you get to a new level.

Manufacturer Information

Company: Bandai America, Inc.
Address: 12951 East 166th Street
         Cerritos, CA
         90701
Telephone: 213-926-0947 (This is a regular toll
         charge telephone call.)
Typical Price: $26.99

Kwirk

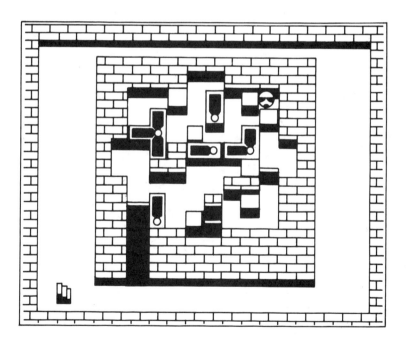

Description

Kwirk is a bodacious tomato with some radical shades, and he's out to get back his girl. She's being held captive somewhere in the city, and Kwirk must run around buildings looking for her. He pushes blocks, whips around turnstiles, and gets a little help from his friends. He hangs out with a pretty healthy bunch, including Curly Carrot, Eddie Eggplant, and Pete the Pepper. This game is perfect for Saturday afternoon vegging. (Sorry!)

Let's Play

The following buttons put you in control of the game, and in command of your vegetables:

■ Identify menu selections.

■ Move up, down, left, or right.

■ When selecting from menus—go to the last section.

■ Start again.

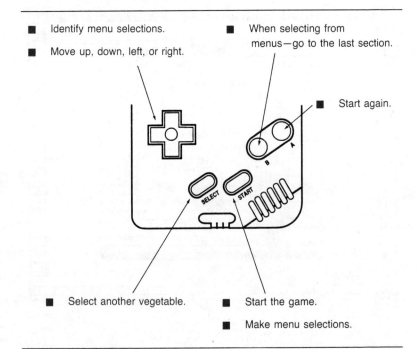

■ Select another vegetable.

■ Start the game.

■ Make menu selections.

You can play any one of the following three games:

Going Up? has floors that you'll need to squeeze your chubby tomato body through.

Heading Out? is a race through maze rooms.

Vs Mode is for two players.

Going Up?

In this game, move up floor by floor or select any floor you like. Select your Skill Level: 1, 2, or 3 (1 is the easiest). Then, select a floor from 1 through 10 (again, 1 is the easiest). Once you've done this, you can choose the display angle. Diagonal View gives a 3-D effect. The Bird's-Eye View is more straightforward. All set? You're ready to start.

In *Going Up?*, anytime you want to start a floor again or end the game, press the A button and make your selection to Redo or End. Sometimes, you'll also get a Back option that will take you back to the previous step. You can back up eight times to retrace your steps. This is especially useful when you get into more complex floors that require many moves. If you accidentally press the A button and see these options, you can press the B button to return to where you left off.

Heading Out?

The theme for *Heading Out?* is "Go West, Young Tomato." The game is a series of connected rooms that continue out to your left—west. They go on and on and on. As soon as you complete one room, the next one comes right at you. You can choose up to 99 rooms in each skill level, so you'll probably never get bored (or done). After picking *Heading Out?*, identify the Skill

Level (1 is easy, 3 is hard). You don't have to play all 99 rooms. You can pick how many rooms you want to work through by pressing a part of the directional button:

- Press left or right to switch between the ones and tens digit.

- Press up or down to increase or decrease the number.

The rooms are selected randomly, so if you choose to play seven rooms on two separate occasions, you probably won't get the same rooms each time.

Once you set the room to start in, identify whether you want the Diagonal (3-D) View or the simpler Bird's-Eye View. Tomato to his mark, and go!

This game is a little difficult to end—you can't press a button and get out. You can turn off your machine. (Ouch! I hate to do that to the software.) Or, you can play to the end. That's the advantage of selecting which room to start with. By selecting a lower number, you have fewer rooms to complete before you get to the end. The number of rooms is displayed along with a graphic gauge of your progress.

When you do get to the end, the top scores are displayed. These are the ones that have registered since the machine was turned on. When you cut the power, *Kwirk* forgets the scores.

Vs Mode

Vs Mode lets two people play the *Heading Out?* game. (Of course, two Game Boys must be connected with the Video Link and you need two *Kwirk* cartridges.) You race against each other to determine the winner. After choosing the *Vs Mode*, the first player to press the Start button gets control of the Selection screen. Just as the regular *Heading Out?*, you pick the Skill Level and the number of rooms you want to play. If one player wants a handicap, you can select fewer rooms for that player. Once the rooms are selected, choose to play the best of 3, 5, 7, or 9 games. After selecting the contest, identify the display angle (Bird's-Eye View is highly recommended).

As you're playing, you can see the progress of both players, including the number of rooms remaining.

Strategies

Hi's Hints

I love *Kwirk*. But, of course, I love being a tomato! I like the fact that you have a lot of control over the difficulty of play, and I like being able to redo mazes in *Heading Out?*. Besides that, it's a blast! The following tips should help you out.

A few obstacles appear over and over again. Get used to them, and you can do anything. The first thing you need to look out for are the brick walls. Don't run into them. Move them? No way. Just avoid them.

You'll also get pretty familiar with turnstiles. These come in four varieties: the single turnstile, the L-shaped, the T-shaped, and the +-shaped. You can usually push a turnstile and spin it to get through, unless a block or wall is in the way.

Although blocks can get in your way, they can come in pretty handy. You can push blocks one by one and use them to fill holes or clear paths, but be sure to plan your moves carefully. If you come to a hole, fill it with a block, and move on. The book says to pick a block that matches the shape of the hole. This is somewhat true. A small block won't fill a big hole. But the big block's effect on small or irregularly shaped holes can be surprising. Check it out!

A good way to learn how to work with walls, turn-stiles, blocks, and holes is to watch the self-running demonstration. Just leave the game on the trademark screen until it times itself out. Then, you'll see the little tomato begin running a *Heading Out?* game. Watch carefully to see how the little master handles the obstacles when left on his own.

I like *Heading Out?*, but *Going Up?* is my favorite just because I can pick the Skill Level and the floor, and because I can restart. If you're a beginner, pick a low Skill Level and easy floors to practice your basic moves. What you learn here will serve you throughout *Kwirk*. For example, in Level 1, Floor 2, you'll see a stack of three blocks. Run in and push the top block all the way to the left; run down and push the bottom block all the way left; then, push the middle block to the bottom and race through. In practice, this whole floor will take you only minutes or seconds to master. Once you've mastered the move, you can use the same pattern in later games in more difficult situations.

Unlike *Heading Out?*, where the rooms are selected randomly, *Going Up?* gives you more control over your selection of levels and floors. For example, if you select Level 1 (easy) and Floor 1, you'll go back to exactly the same floor, not a random floor. If you want to master a particular floor before moving on to the next one, you can keep replaying the floor again and again. If you're matching scores with a friend, you can trick him into picking a level and floor that you've mastered, and waste him!

To master *Heading Out?*, you need to figure out the pattern that'll get you to the stairs at the far end of the screen. If you only have the tomato, the game's pretty simple; use your vine-ripened hero to push the blocks. No pulling in this game. Just pushing.

If you have another vegetable, the game's more fun (and more complicated). You can put one vegetable in position, push the block on top of that vegetable, and let him take over. This allows for some moves that one vegetable (no matter how virile) could handle alone. Level 1,

Floor 6 is the first opportunity you'll get to use the two-vegetable technique. When you get there, try this: Put the tomato in the far left bottom. When you press Select, he stops pounding his foot and the other veggie starts pulsing. Have that pulsing veggie put the box on the head of the tomato. Give one push up with the tomato. Use the other veggie to push the block over the hole, and run both veggies through. Ahh, teamwork!

One caution: Teamwork is great, but you also have more veggies to worry about. When you have multiple vegetables, you have to get all of them to the stairs. You can't just sacrifice a carrot to save your pepper. When you're getting one guy through the maze, make sure you're not boxing in another.

Before you get started in *Going Up?*, study the maze. Always. Running around and flipping turnstiles is a good way to get frustrated and consume time, but that's about it. Instead, try to picture in your mind how the turnstiles will turn. When you have an idea of how you want to attack the maze, try it out. If you're close but not quite successful, you can always start the floor over right away. What you've just learned will be fresh in your mind.

You'll want to play with turnstiles a bit to see how they relate to one another. The more you do it, the more you'll see patterns and build your skill. Often, you have to run around and position turnstiles in advance. This is known as a back-end run. Do that, then make your final, winning moves.

Although the game keeps track of time and the number of steps it takes you to get to the stairs, don't worry about it at first. The game won't bomb you out. After you've mastered the basics, you can start worrying about fine-tuning your game.

By the way, when you select a floor, you have your choice of views. The Diagonal View shows a 3-D effect from above, complete with shadows. The Bird's-Eye View shows the same top view without 3-D and shadows. I prefer the Bird's-Eye view—in the Diagonal View, the holes sometimes get lost in the shadows.

Tec's Tips

In any Kwirk game, keep in mind that there's always a way to solve it. Don't get frustrated. You may push a box all the way left then down to fill a hole, only to find out that your passage doesn't get through to the end. Don't get mad—try a new approach. Try pushing the box halfway left, then down, then all the way left. Violà! It works. Moral: Try it from a different direction or with a new twist.

How blocks fill holes can be deceiving. If you have a large hole, try moving the block to different positions; you'll eventually find the position that fills the hole. Push the blocks around a little and play with the position of the veggie. In Level 1, Floor 4, for example, there's only one large block and a large hole. If you use the tomato to press the block down then left on the top right corner of the block, you won't fill the hole. But if the tomato makes the final push from the bottom right corner of the block, the block clicks right into place, and the hole is filled.

Take it easy. If you move too fast, you'll hit into things that you should be trying to avoid. A gentle tap, tap, tap on the directional button will get you wherever you're going quick enough.

Take your time and plan your moves before you run around and wear yourself out. It doesn't matter how much time you take when you don't know how to get through the maze anyway. If you get in a toot, you may shove a block against a wall and really get yourself in a jam. You'll lose a lot of time at the beginning planning moves, but it's worth it. Once you figure out your strategy, then you can go for speed.

Also, be gentle. Some boxes can only be pushed so far. Some holes are as stubborn as brick walls. If you get into a shoving match with a brick wall or a hole, you'll probably be the one to lose.

You can rarely, if ever, just flip through turnstiles to get from one end of the game to the other. You have to set them up just right so that when you turn the next one, it opens a clear path to the end.

I prefer *Heading Out?*, but I think that's just because I like to destroy Hi a lot. When you get to an area you can't get through, just press the A button to free yourself. Your minutes, score, or bonus won't reset, and you can try again.

One really neat thing about *Heading Out?* is that you can go back and start over on a floor by pressing the A button, then selecting Redo. If you mess up, you can adjust your strategy and try again while it's fresh in your mind. This lets you develop a strategy rather than forcing you to re-invent it every time.

Heading Out? bonus points start at 2,000. 100 points evaporate every 10 seconds. If you get the room solved within 1 minute and 20 seconds, you get to keep the remaining bonus points.

Other Pointers

- You may push a block into a large hole, only to find that it doesn't create a path. You can push the block across as long as you have a path to push from. If you can't push any more, get another block to make a path, and keep pushing.

- Sometimes the best strategy when you're stuck is to eliminate the moves that won't work. This leaves you with a limited set of alternatives to try.

- You'll tend to see the shortest move as the best option. Slow down. The long way around may be better. What if you go all the way around and get that block or turnstile from the opposite side? Think about it. Consider the less obvious alternatives.

- You may need to move a block out of your way, go around it, then put it back where it was. You'll see plenty of examples of this in *Heading Out?* Level 1, Floor 8. In this floor, it's a matter of getting on the other side of the block, making sure the path is clear, then pushing the block back to the right. Remember, you only need a corner of a block to push it.

- *Heading Out?*—Want the thrill of cleaning up a floor real fast? Press the A button and Redo just before you hit the stairs. You'll get a chance to do it again and eventually race through the floor.

- If you're playing for score (versus just solving the puzzle), it's important to note that time and wasted moves hurt your score.

Manufacturer Information

Company: Acclaim Entertainment, Inc.
Address: 71 Audrey Avenue
         Oyster Bay, New York
         11771
Acclaim Hotline: 516-624-9300 (This is a regular toll
         charge telephone call.)
Typical Price: $27.99

Malibu Beach Volleyball

Description

Hey, dudes, get out your jams and bikinis, and get ready for a radical round of Malibu Beach Volleyball. This is no bump-it-over-the-net, "Mr. Nice Guy" game, but real spike-and-dig, beach-scene volleyball.

Let's Play

Use the following controls to block, slam, and spike your way to victory:

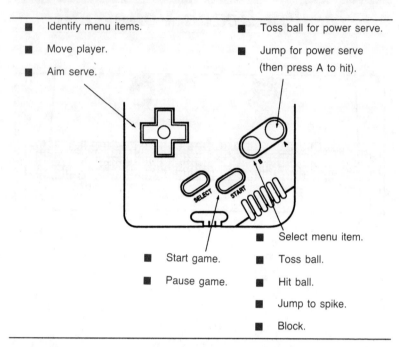

- Identify menu items.
- Move player.
- Aim serve.

- Toss ball for power serve.
- Jump for power serve (then press A to hit).

- Select menu item.

- Start game.
- Pause game.

- Toss ball.
- Hit ball.
- Jump to spike.
- Block.

You can play with one or two players. In a three-game match, you need to win two out of three 12-point games to claim victory. Play one game, and you need to score 15. To keep things fair, you change sides when the score is a multiple of 8. In either game, you have to win by two points.

Strategies

Hi's Hints

Practice a little with an easy game first. Play the USA women's team against Italy—the activity is slower. To play successfully against the computer, you'll need quite a bit of practice, even when you're the USA and the other team is Italy. It takes some time to learn where to move your players to return the ball. You'll have to work on your timing when it comes to serves.

When you begin serving, stick to the basic serve. Just hit the A button twice (once to toss the ball and once to hit it). For the intermediate player, use the regular serve and try to aim the ball. Hit it down the line or in the corner. To aim, press the left or right arrow while hitting the A button the second time. Only advanced players should try the power serve. The timing is difficult, but with practice, you can get it down. The standard rules of volleyball apply:

- If you goof up your serve, it's side out—the other team gets to serve.

- When your opponent serves, you have up to three hits to return the ball.

- The same player can't hit the ball two times in a row.

- You score only on your serve.

It's not all that easy to control your players, so when you start out, just try to get the ball over the net.

Tec's Tips

Spike and block. The only team you'll beat by bumping the ball over the net is the Italians. The Brazilians are pretty fast, so if you try that sissy stuff on them, they'll cream you. The Japanese are good spikers—they'll hammer the ball right down your throat, so try to get up there and block it back, or hang back and try to dig it out of the sand. Stay on your toes. The USA team is the best, so you have an advantage throughout the tournament.

To spike, press the B button to jump. When you get to the top of your jump, press the A button to drill the ball over the net. If you miss your timing at the top, you'll hit it out or smash the ball right into the net.

Try spiking with more than one player. Use one player to bump the ball up into position. When the ball is in just the right spot, jump with another player and slam the ball over the net. This kind of spike requires a little accuracy in the passing, but it makes the game a lot of fun. You may find it easier to use three hits—pass twice, and spike. This is a little more difficult to execute, but it gets the ball in a better position for the spike.

If the opponent tries to spike, block it. Run up to the net, and press the B button. Get your timing right, and they'll be eating sand. It's pretty difficult to dig a blocked shot.

Digging consists of getting under the ball when it's hit hard and low—you have to "dig" the ball out of the sand. Be quick. Move in the right direction. Don't go for the opponent's fake. Sometimes you have to anticipate. Pick a direction and start running—you have a 50/50 chance of making the right move. Often the ball will look like it's in the sand when it's not. Keep at it, and you can make some pretty cool digs.

When you do a dig, you usually don't hit the ball hard enough to get it over the net—you're just trying to get the ball out of the sand. So don't forget to run your second player into position to hit the ball.

As you get more advanced, try to hit the ball two or three times to get it over the net. You'll fake out your opponent and score more points. But be careful. Hit the ball four times, and the other team gets the ball, and maybe the point.

The two-player, power volley ball is the most exciting mode of play. You'll win more points with power serves and spikes than you will by just bumping the ball over. Also, dinking (just barely tipping it over the net) is not part of this game. The unspoken rule of the beach says no dinking in two-man ball. If you dink, you may as well trade in your jams and put on a three-piece suit.

Other Pointers

- The secret of volleyball is to hit it where they ain't.

- If you're playing a two-player game, handicap the game by giving USA to the weaker player and Italy to the very skilled player.

- Move your position back and forth when you serve. This will help catch your challengers flat footed.

- If the opponent is spiking, send a player right up to block. Get up right in their face, and you'll score.

- A dig usually requires more than one hit. Keep your players ready.

Manufacturer Information

Company: Activision
Address: P.O. Box 3048
        Menlo Park, CA
        94025
Telephone: 415-329-7699 (This is a regular toll charge telephone call.) 8:30 a.m. to 5:00 p.m. Pacific time.
Typical Price: $24.99

Motocross Maniacs

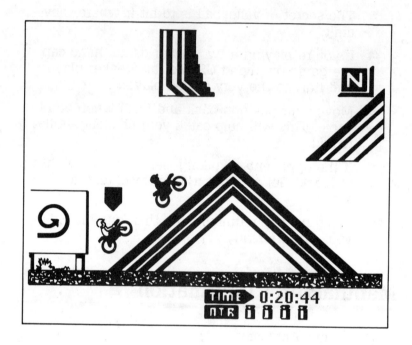

Description

It's dirt track time. Take your souped up, turbo-boosted
bike over rocks, around loops, and across country. Forget
what Mom told you about taking it easy on the bikes.
Keep your foot on the throttle, your hands on the grips,
and tear up the track! This game is so fast, you'll need to
scrape the bugs off your teeth when it's over.

Let's Play

Use the following controls to flip, jump, and fly around the track:

■   Control position of bike.

■   Up during jump to go high.

■   Right in the air to flip.

■   Left on the ground to do wheelie.

■   Choose modes.   Nitro Turbo Boost!

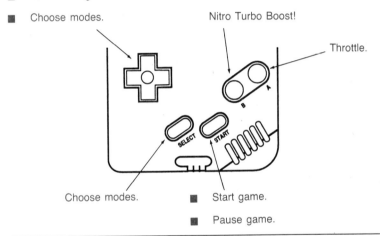

Throttle.

Choose modes.   ■ Start game.

■ Pause game.

When you first start the game, you'll need to choose the mode of play. Here they are:

Lone Wolf Solo Mode—you race against the clock.

Computer Challenge Mode—race against a super fine computer foe.

Maniac-A-Maniac Two Player Mode—make your buddy eat your dust.

On the bottom of your screen you'll see the maximum speed, the time limit, and the number of Nitro Canisters you have left.

In single play *Motocross Maniacs*, you get to choose from three levels of play: A, B, and C. Level A gives you the most time to complete each course; Level C gives you the least. In each level are eight different courses.

To maximize your skill and control, you can hold the Game Boy in either of two ways. One way is to use your left thumb to control the directional button and your middle and index fingers to control the A and B buttons. The other way is to keep your left thumb on the directional button and use your right thumb to press the A and B buttons. The dual thumb method is more tiring, and the thumb-finger method is more awkward. Use the one that's most effective for you.

As you cruise down the course, you'll want to pick up the following objects:

N   *Nitro Turbo Boosts* for explosive power.

S   *Maximum Speed Multiplier* to amplify your speed.

R   *Radial Tires* to grip the road.

T   *Bonus Time* to add 10 seconds to your clock.

J   *Jet Propulsion Fuel* to add power to the Turbo Boost when you're in the air. You'll find this fuel when you flip your bike in the air at certain points in the course.

   Mini-Maniacs just for fun.

In this game, you'll go through loops, bumps, macho dirt, and hop-a-long jumps. You'll get caught between some rocks and hard places (pop a wheelie and use a Nitro Burst to get out). You'll encounter bowl-dacious obstacles, and radical ramps. Enough? It's never enough!

Strategies

Hi's Hints

If you're just starting out, stick with Course 1, Level A. As you improve, the computer will automatically move you up to the next level.

The toughest part of any course is the rocks. Sometimes one lone rock will seem to pop up at you from out of the track. Other times a long string of rocks will appear, complete with ramps and low ceilings. If you have trouble weaving between these rocks, you should stay on the lower courses and practice. When you get to the higher levels, the play speeds up, and these rock trails get to be a real pain. The only way to get good at this is to practice the ramps, jumps, and loops until you get a feel for them. And the best place to practice is in the lower levels, where the game play is relatively slow.

Keep a finger or thumb on the A button to keep your speed up. Also, keep your thumb on the top part of the directional control and press the left or right side nice and easy when needed. The reason? You'll get the most distance out of your jumps and the same time be able to control the tilt of the motorcycle.

It's easy to lose control of your bike. Be careful when popping wheelies. Once you start to tumble, you'll have to stop moving before the game will give you back control of your bike. Don't wipe out. When you do, you lose everything you worked so hard to gain—all of the objects that you may have picked up (except Nitro Turbo Boosts) and any Bonus Time.

You can usually pick up Mini-Maniacs at the beginning of the course, but they don't really serve much purpose. To pick one up, you have to do a midair somersault while riding on the upper courses. Use the same technique to pick up Jet Propulsion Fuel. Look for the fuel over two Hop-A-Long jumps somewhere in the middle of the courses. Go for it.

Tec's Tips

If you have plenty of Nitro Turbo Boosts, use them to maintain top speed and pick up the available objects in the loops and bowls. But don't use too many—you may need them to get out of some tough situations later.

Try the Turbo Boosts on hills. If you're going downhill, kick in a Turbo Boost—now you're jammin'! Try it on the uphill too, when you start losing speed. If you see two rocks in a row, try this: Use a Turbo Boost to jump the first one and bounce off the second. In Course 8, you'll get to do it two times in a row!

I like to use the jets to fly over everything, but be on guard. You never know what may happen way up in the air. You can make up a lot of time staying in the air, but you have to keep an eye on how many fuel canisters you have left.

It's a fun game. Share it with a friend.

Other Pointers

- If you find yourself getting stuck in the Macho Dirt a lot, try pushing up on the directional button when going off the end of the ramps and jumps.

- When you're about to land on the back side of a jump, make sure you're parallel to the jump. If you're off a little, you'll wipe out, and you won't get control of your bike till you tumble to the bottom.

- Pop a wheelie to go over rocks and stones.

Manufacturer Information

Company: Ultra Software Corporation
Address: 900 Deerfield Parkway
Buffalo Grove, Illinois
60089-4510
Telephone: 708-215-5111 (This is a regular toll
charge telephone call.)
Typical Price: $24.99

Nemesis

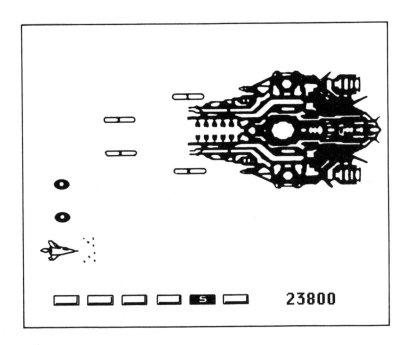

Description

Jump in your spaceship, strap yourself in, and fire up the afterburners. You're in hot pursuit of the evil King Nemesis and his band of alien scum. You fly through the cosmos with a single companion, super Proteus 911, a weapon that has the firepower to turn an entire planet into cosmic dust. But watch out; you're not the only starfighter in the galaxy!

Let's Play

Use the following buttons to control your flight and to fire your weapons:

■ Move Starship.

■ Up/down—move through Configuration screen.

■ Right/left—change values on Configuration screen.

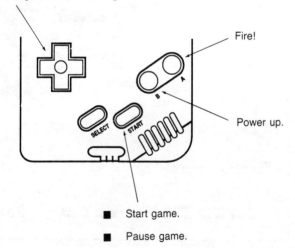

Fire!

Power up.

■ Start game.

■ Pause game.

You'll need to fly through the following five stages before your final encounter with Nemesis:

Carnage Canyon

Pyramids of Pyromania

Lair of the Planetary Pirates

Den of Doom and Gloom

Sacrificial Sarcophagus of Saturn

You can pick any of these five stages through the Configuration screen. After picking the stage, choose the level of play—Level 1 for beginners or Level 2 for more advanced play. This screen also lets you choose the number of ships you want to start out with. The number is shown in the REST field. Hold down the directional control, and you can start the game with up to 99 ships. This gives you a lot of life.

The AUTOSHOT option gives you continuous shooting power when it is ON or single shot power when it is OFF. Start out with autoshot. You can switch to single shot when you get the hang of the game. Finally, you can set the SHOT/POWER UP option to identify the button (A or B) for each. Shot is for firing your normal weapon. Once you have a power-up capsule, you can use the button you identify as POWER UP for shooting the missiles, double gun, and laser.

In addition to killing alien ships and bosses, you should try to nail the following four capsules:

Enemy annihilation capsule—Get this capsule and all the aliens will be destroyed.

Bonus stage capsule—These capsules are only in the bonus stage. Capture them all and you'll get a special surprise. (Entrances to the bonus stages are hidden throughout the game.)

1-UP capsule—Look for these capsules only in the bonus stage. Each capsule gives you an additional ship. (As if you needed more ships!)

◇ *Power-up capsule*—These guys are found all over in the game. Drive into them, and the Proteus 911 powers up. Your level of power is shown on the bottom of the screen: S for speed, M for missiles, D for double gun, L for laser, O for option destructive device, and F for force field.

Strategies

 ### Hi's Hints

Nemesis is a lot like the games you see in an arcade. Pick your level, give yourself lots of spaceships for a good, long game, and go to it! As you get more skilled, play the higher levels, and start out with fewer ships. Remember, you can always get more.

When you're fighting, hold down the shoot button the entire time and keep moving back and forth with the directional control. You might get lucky. Alien aircraft may approach from the edge of the screen, and you can bag them by mistake.

In general, move up and down the screen, so you can see all enemies. Stay a little to the left—this will give you the most visibility. Gun turrets along the edge of the screen will shoot at you. Don't ignore them.

You can move and bump up against the edge of the screen without dying, but don't hit into a mountain. If you do, you're dead.

Bad dudes will come up from behind, usually from the bottom rather than the middle. In other words, you can't just park yourself on the left and stay there. You need to keep moving. When you're trying to get away, don't get trapped by the edge of the screen. If you do, you won't be able to wiggle your way out.

All of the aliens move and shoot in specific patterns. As you encounter new aliens, try to figure out their patterns, then fry them.

Each stage has an Alien Crime Master. In Stage 1, it's Intergalactic Super Force. To kill this guy, keep blasting away.

Tec's Tips

Watch your side. If you get hit from the side, you're a goner. If you're dodging some big old monster and it brushes against your side, you're a goner. In other words, try to attack your enemies head on. In the case of the monster, you might have a chance if you shoot exactly when the monster touches your side, but don't count on it.

The bad guys are specially trained to avoid your skinny bullets. If you think you got 'em all, don't be too sure. You may have just missed one in the last wave of enemy fire. He'll fly up from the side, and you can kiss another spaceship good-bye.

Basically speaking, the bigger the enemy, the more times you have to hit it to kill it.

There is no way to shoot backwards, so don't fly past something that's likely to catch you. Destroy it instead. Sometimes the enemy will come out of nowhere and attack from behind. Try to get the position on him, and waste him. You'll need to play Roger-dodger.

When you die, you aren't always sent back to the beginning of the screen. If you've passed a certain point, you will start off further in the level.

Aliens know where you are. They don't just attack at random. So you can't just sit in one spot and try to ambush them. Keep moving. Dodge the onslaught. Divide and conquer!

Go for capsules. The enemy annihilation capsule comes up fairly often, and it's most useful. Don't waste it, though. Wait till you're surrounded by the enemy, till there's no way out. Then, let 'er rip. The enemies won't know what hit them. The 1-UP capsule is helpful if you didn't start out with a bunch of ships. When you're getting low on ships, these capsules look mighty fine.

The power-up capsule gives you several alternatives. Get that power-up, and you can use the B button to give yourself more speed or to change from your normal weapon to some more advanced firepower. Hit the power-up capsule the first time, and you get the speed burner. Hit it again, and you get the missiles. The speed burner and missiles are both very helpful. The double gun is one of the best because it gets so many shots off. If you don't get up to the laser, you'll have a tough time defeating the big, bad guys at the end.

You can't use all of the powers at the same time (for example, you can't use both the laser and double gun because they both involve shooting). The force field keeps you from running into objects, but you should develop this skill yourself. The extra shooting powers are much more helpful. If you kill the guy, you don't have to worry so much about defending yourself from his fire.

You won't always want to hit into a power-up capsule and start using the next weapon. Sometimes the lesser weapons are more effective.

Fly along, minding your own business, and suddenly you'll be in a bonus stage. The bonus stage can get you a lot of points. If you get them all, a big, BIG bonus comes your way.

Other Pointers

- If you have the force field and you get hit three times, you no longer have the force field.

- Capture the power-up capsules. Go for killer shooting ability.

Manufacturer Information

Company: Ultra Software Corporation
Address: 900 Deerfield Parkway
Buffalo Grove, IL
60089-4510
Telephone: 708-215-5111 (This is a regular toll
charge telephone call.)
Typical Price: $24.95

NFL Football

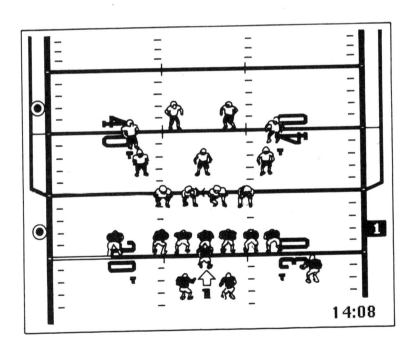

Description

Ready to hunker in a huddle with the Goliaths of the NFL? Then get ready for the Game Boy version of *NFL Football*! In this version, you'll be planning strategies and butting helmets with the best in the league. Pick the dirt off your face mask, swagger up to the line, and listen to the count. On two—Hut! Hut!

Let's Play

Whether you're passing, punting, or diving for the interception, you'll need to use the following controls:

■ Identify selections.　　■ Identify receiver.

■ Move active player.　　■ Change defensive player.

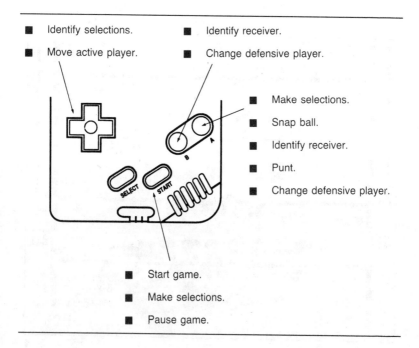

■ Make selections.

■ Snap ball.

■ Identify receiver.

■ Punt.

■ Change defensive player.

■ Start game.

■ Make selections.

■ Pause game.

NFL Football follows the rules of professional football. You get four plays to move the ball ten yards for a first down. You can move the ball on the ground or in the air —the choice is yours. Get the ball across the goal line, and you score a TD (touchdown). Kick it through the uprights for a field goal.

You can choose between a long game or a short game by setting the clock for normal (15 minutes) or short (10 minutes).

After you set the game clock, pick your team. Unfortunately the game provides no statistics. Each team's style of play is similar to that of the corresponding real-life team, but you should try them all out to see which one suits your style of play.

The arrow on the screen points to the player you're controlling.

Strategies

Hi's Hints

On offense, you can set up in any of six formations: the slot T, the pro T, the shot gun, the T, the Y, and the I formation. If you're on your end of the field, go with a more conservative formation. Put several blockers up front, and don't split your receivers. The tighter patterns like the Y formation or the T, the pro T, or slot T work well. Personally, I like the shot gun—it gives you a lot of options. By staying tight on your end of the field, you protect yourself against losing yardage.

If you're an expert player, figure out a play, then practice it till you have it down pat. Although it's important to mix plays up and keep the other team guessing, it never hurts to have a bread-and-butter play. There's no coach on the other sideline saying "Hey, they're running the shot gun every time!" Run the play, and make the most of its options.

Watch the on-screen statistics at all times. These stats show the score, the time remaining, yards to go, and other information that might help you decide which play to run. Use this information to decide whether you'll go short or long or whether you want to run or pass. If you're behind with 30 seconds left, you don't want to be running up the middle.

To look through the play options, press the directional control down. When the highlight is on the play you want, press the A button to choose the play.

As you run the play, you have options. On a pass play, for example, you'll see the A and B receivers on the screen. Those are the ones you can throw to, if you're going to throw. As a quarterback, you can always bootleg and keep on going. For the beginner, run for a while. After that, you can start trying to throw the ball.

Complete the throw, and you're in luck—a pass play can net you some good yardage. But if it's intercepted, you're suddenly on defense, and you can get in a lot of trouble. On your end of the field, go more with running plays to prevent an interception deep in your own territory. When you get to their end of the field, open up your passing game. When you get close to the goal line, everyone starts to get packed in real tight. Passing and running are both difficult, but it's really tough to get the ball to a receiver.

Tec's Tips

You'll need to learn two important things: how close you can get to a defender without getting tackled and how to throw the ball.

If it's fourth down and you have more than two yards to go for a first, you probably should punt or try a field goal, unless you really need to score a touchdown. Trying to throw on fourth and long is difficult. If you're deep in your own territory, punt.

Use the A button to control the distance of your punt. It takes some practice. Don't worry about flubbing the first few—it'll be like handing the ball to the other team. After a while, you'll get your technique down pat.

When you're inside the opponent's 40 yard line and select the punt option, the game automatically sets you up to kick a field goal. All the punting practice you've gotten will prepare you for kicking the three-pointer.

If you try to run on every play, the defense will wise up real quick and shut you down. You need to mix in at least a few passes. To pass to receiver A, press the A button. To pass to receiver B, press B. The closer you are, the easier it is to complete your pass. If you pass straight down field, you're more likely to complete the pass than if you try to go across the field.

If you complete a pass, you automatically get control of the receiver. Be on your toes. Get that guy moving toward the goal line.

This is a high-scoring game. If you don't score, the computer will make up the difference. In other words, don't rely on your defense to shut down the opposition.

On defense, you have a choice of seven defense alignments: 5-2, 5-3-3, 3-5-3, 4-3-4, 4-4-3, 6-2, and the goal-line stand. The numbers represent the defensive layout; for example, a 5-3-3 is five men on the line, three linebackers, and three men out in the secondary.

The goal-line stand places all your men up close to the line of scrimmage. Use it on short-yardage situations, such as fourth and one or close to the goal line. The idea is to get up in their faces and jam the offensive linemen right at the line of scrimmage. If the line gets a good head of steam, the runner will probably get the necessary yardage. The goal line stand is also useful on third and short or fourth and short if the opposing team decides to go for it.

The 5-2 and the 4-3-4 have two safeties. In passing situations, it's nice to have those safeties back there. In long-yardage situations, the other team will probably try to pass. These defenses will give you a good chance at stopping them.

All the information about your defense appears on the screen. Use this information to determine your strategy before starting the play. The best defense to use depends on what play the offense calls. For example, if the offense calls a running play, and you're set up with only three guys on the line, they'll probably burst right through your middle. Keep track of how many men you have close to the line, how many are back from the line, and how spread out you are. You'll have to trust your luck a little, but try to play as smart as possible.

The defense is star oriented. Regardless of which defensive alignment you select, you control one man, and your man has to make the tackle. The other ten guys only slow down the play for you. You can change the player you control with the A or B button. Keep changing players till the ball is snapped. That way, you'll confuse the offense and have a better chance at shutting them down.

Don't let the guy you're controlling get too close to the other defensive players. If you do, you risk getting tripped up by your own players. Also, don't get too close or too far from the line of scrimmage. When the ball is snapped, you have to move. If you're too far from the line, you'll have a long way to go to get the guy with the ball. Get too close, and you'll get jammed at the line. Then, you have to go backwards and run around the end to get to the ball.

Try using a cornerback or linebacker as your star player. If the offense needs short to medium yardage, you ought to use a linebacker. If it's longer yardage and you suspect a pass, you can use a cornerback or safety to cover the receiver. Don't give up too much yardage, or you'll never get their offense in trouble. Take a chance. Pick someone close to the line, and try to anticipate the offense. You might just throw them for a loss.

There's a lot of guesswork on defense. You need to think ahead. Think of what play you would run in a similar situation, and set up your defense accordingly. A surprise move may work, but playing smart is best in the long run.

Other Pointers

- Practice moving your defensive man, to keep him from getting bottled up or boxed in.

- Between the quarters, the game may appear to stop. Press the A or B button to move on to the next quarter.

- As in real football, it's tough to go against the grain—that is, across the field. If you throw against the grain, you'll throw interceptions. Run against the grain, and you'll run into packs of defenders. If you have a choice to run straight ahead for a couple yards or run through an opening against the grain, take the couple yards.

Manufacturer Information

Company: Konami Inc.
Address: 900 Deerfield Parkway
         Buffalo Grove, Illinois
         60089-4510
Telephone: 708-215-5111 (This is a regular toll charge telephone call.)
Typical Price: $24.95

Revenge of the 'Gator

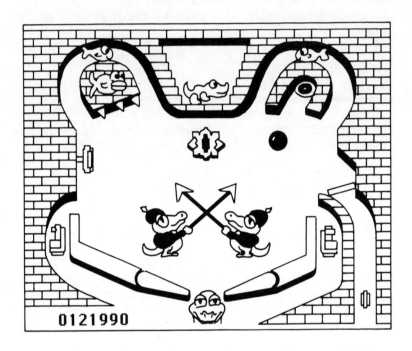

0121990

Description

From the three little 'gators who dance at the bottom of
the screen through the four exciting pinball levels, you'll
find *Revenge of the 'Gator* one of the most playful games
around. If your ball slip slides away, a 'gator gobbles it
up. If you smack a 'gator in it's gaping mouth, the ball is
a goner. Sometimes, though, 'gators are your cronies and
they help out by batting your ball with their tails. Get a
correct toss and you're in secret-level land. Pinball wiz-
ards will get a bang outta this one. Have fun, ya'all.

Let's Play

Use the following buttons to take control of 'gator land:

■ Choose menu items.   ■ Hold either button then release to shoot ball.

■ Move left flipper.   ■ Use either button to flip the right flipper.

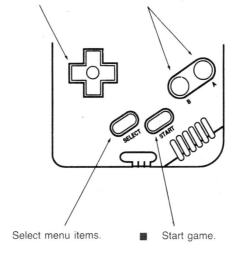

Select menu items.   ■ Start game.

■ Pause game.

The 'gator is revenging with four games for your pin-ball pleasure:

'Gator 1 Player—for a person playing alone.

'Gator 2 Players—for two players.

Matchplay A—for two entry-level players.

Matchplay B—for two master players.

In matchplay, turn on the two Game Boys at the same time. The goal in matchplay is to lower your pal's score by hitting the targets on his or her side. Get them to zero and you win. In match play, you can strike a few items that will cause some fun stuff to happen. A pill with a number is a score. Three dancing 'gators reverses the scores. Circles with letters or symbols mean the following:

G—Ball gets heavy as a rock.

F—A flipper goes away.

S—Savers (blocks of exits) show up.

||—Blocks appear in the center.

←—Gravity goes up.

R—Return to normal play before special power.

'Gator and Crossbones—Ball goes over and the game is done.

Just select your game and get going by holding down the A or B button and releasing it. A quick punch of the button won't be enough oomph to get it going. Experiment with your release.

The score screen comes up when the game is over (you done got ate, honey child). The score shows the top score along with 1P (1st player) and 2P (2nd player) scores.

If you're good as a greased 'gator, you can put your initials among the top five by using the directional button to identify letters then Select to make the selection.

If you want to take a little break, press Start during play to see the score. Press Start again to continue.

Strategies

Hi's Hints

'Gators galore. It's kind of funky, but if you like pinball or games that mix a lot of skill with a lot of chance, you'll like *Revenge of the 'Gator.*

This jumbo pinball machine offers four levels of play: Screen A, B, C, and D. You'll also encounter three bonus screens and a screen where the bad 'gator swallows your ball—gulp! As your ball moves from one level to the next, the screen flashes. (My brother thought this flashing meant the game was broken when he first turned it on.)

When you release the ball, it goes to the middle of the playing board (Screen C). You'll become real familiar with this screen. Hit those little nubs on the left wall, and the gate above (which leads to the upper screens) opens. Run over the position to make each of four hearts across the top appear. Side savers and the saver post show up to give you a big advantage. When the center lights flash, smack the bumpers for high points. The upper right loop causes the slot machine squares in the center to spin. If you get three stars, your bonus multiplier increases. Get three fish, and all the savers show up for easy play. If you get three symbols that look like peppers, you lose savers and your bonus multiplier goes back to 1000x1. To get to higher screens, you can try to get up by going straight through the ceiling (good luck getting past the barriers) or by knocking out the door in the upper left and getting into the passageway.

In Screen A, hit fish and then hit the 'gator when it's released for a free ball. The drop targets in the upper left are pretty easy to get, and they give you saver posts. Smack the ball into the upper left slot, and, congratulations, you're in Bonus Stage 3—50,000 points for each 'gator you hit.

89

In Screen B you just want to hit, hit, hit. Kill all the stuff on the left, and you go to Bonus Stage 2, where you get 30,000 points for each 'gator you hit. Do the same on the right, and you'll go to Screen A. The 'gators in the center grow, savers show, then they go.

Once you're past the first pair of paddles going down, you're in Screen D. My favorite play is to flatten the noses of the 'gators on the left. The first time you do it, savers come up. The second time, the mouths of the three at the top stay open. Going into the left 'gator's mouth puts you back up a screen. Venture into the far right 'gator's mouth and you wind up in the shooter lane. Go into the center 'gator's mouth and you're in Bonus Stage 1, which ain't bad. Hit a 'gator as he drops, and you get a whopping 10,000 points!

Three of the bonus rounds are a little tough to get to—you'll have to hit some special targets. In each bonus round, go for the 'gators. You may see one running across the top of the screen or several in a circle. The young ones may be just hatching! No matter how cute they look—nail 'em!

As a general rule, score items on the side are almost always better than score items in the middle.

Try to keep that ball up high. When you're down low, you don't have time to react, and the ball is liable to slip away. Try swinging late to hit the ball off the tip of the paddle. This sends the ball off on a better angle and flips it higher than if you swing early and hit the ball with the middle of the paddle.

Tec's Tips

The 'gator comes into play with his appetite for goofed shots. Muff a shot, and the 'gator gobbles it up. The game is full of 'gators, and the general goal is to whack them in the face with the ball and get points. I do a lot of that, so when he inevitably bites me at the end, I have the secret laugh.

General pinball strategies apply in this game. The most important is to stay away from trouble. You'll run into the most trouble at the bottom level—that's where the 'gator eats your ball and you lose it. Stay at the top and get into the higher levels.

Keep toward the sides of the screen. Don't aim at obstacles in the middle of the screen. If you do, you'll be more likely to rack up a lot of strikes; that is, the machine will just throw the ball right down the middle, and there's no way to hit it with either paddle. If you hit goodies on the edge, the ball tends to bounce around and you have a better chance of getting another swipe at the ball.

In terms of hitting the ball, you want to hit late. Late means hitting the ball off the end of the paddle. If you hit it in the middle of the paddle, it goes in the middle of the screen. If you hit it late, it runs off at an angle toward the other side. All the fun stuff, all the points, and all the ways to get up to the higher parts of the game are off at the edges of the screen. So, if you hit it late, you're more likely to win.

Speaking of the side of the screen, you may notice patterns or groups of objects. You may see two or three targets in row. Usually, if you get all the targets in one zone, you'll get a special surprise. You might get a 'gator head that sits between your paddles and keeps the ball from dropping through. If you get this "gate," keep an eye on him—when he's just about ready to disappear, he'll blink. These special surprises are usually defensive items that keep you from getting strikes.

There's one exception to the hit late rule. If the ball is coming toward your paddle, and you want to aim at a target that's on the same side of the screen as that paddle, hit the ball early, very early.

If you're in trouble, don't fiddle around with just one paddle—dig, dig, dig. Go with the left and the right and the left and the right. Even though you don't plan it, many times the ball will fly out of there. If the ball is way out at the end, you may need to hit it several times to dig it out. Dig it out, and you're back in the game.

Remember, this is electronic pinball, not mechanical pinball. You can't lean against it with your body and make it tilt, or move the game and control the ball. No matter how hard you whack it while you play, it won't tilt (you'll only harm your Game Boy). It's tempting to move the machine a little when the ball is hovering in a spot. But resist. Messing with the angle of the machine is just a waste of time. Speed and accuracy are the keys.

Don't worry about the fact that the high score is 500,000. You'll have to play quite a while to get that much. If you find yourself getting one or two hundred thousand, you're playing pretty good *'Gator*.

Other Pointers

- Don't get mesmerized by what's going on in other parts of the screen. Some of the movements cause a domino effect, and you may be tempted to take your eyes off your ball and pay attention to the spinning squares or gate flippers. While you stray, your ball is heading for trouble. Keep your eye on the ball.

- You can only get one free ball per game. After that, the bonus multiplier is increased.

Manufacturer Information

Company: HAL America Inc.
Address: 7873 S. W. Cirrus 25-F
         Beaverton, Oregon
         97005
Telephone: 503-644-4117 (This is a regular toll
         charge telephone call.)
Typical Price: $26.99

SolarStriker

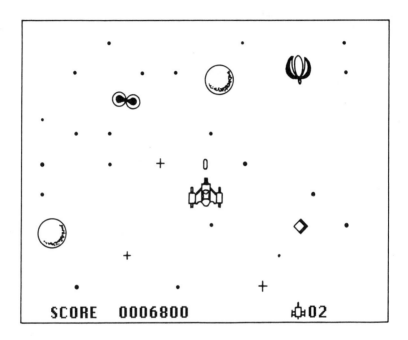

Description

It's 2159. The enemy planet, Reticulon, has built an intergalactic weapon system and is bent on taking over the
earth. Your mission—get to the enemy planet's core base
and destroy it. The odds are against you. You have only
three ships to fight against thousands of enemy ships.
But with a little help from Hi and Tec, you can destroy
the core base, save the earth, and rescue the galaxy from
the Reticulon tyrants.

Let's Play

Use the following buttons to control your ship and fire
your weapons:

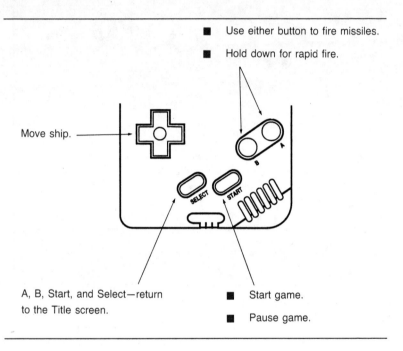

■ Use either button to fire missiles.

■ Hold down for rapid fire.

Move ship.

A, B, Start, and Select—return
to the Title screen.

■ Start game.

■ Pause game.

SolarStriker has six stages:

1. *Steller Area.*

2. *Ozone.*

3. *City.*

4. *Death Valley.*

5. *Outer Base.*

6. *Core of Base.*

Your screen displays your score and the number of ships you have left.

 There are four missile power levels. Hit the power-up item to go to the next level:

1. Single shot.

2. Double shot.

3. Triple shot.

4. Turbo missiles.

If your SolarStriker ship gets shot out of the air, your missile power decreases by one level. A new SolarStriker is awarded you for every 50,000 points. The scoring goes like this:

■ 200 points for each power-up item.

■ 1000 points for a power-up item that you hit with a turbo missile.

■ 200 to 500 points for hitting enemies.

■ 1000 points for the Terra Cannon enemy.

Strategies

Hi's Hints

Firing expertise is a must in this game. Keep a finger on the fire button instead of moving your fingers rapidly to shoot. It's also easier to use one finger (generally the thumb) to move your ship into position for an attack.

When firing, try to hit the enemy ships as high on the screen as possible. Sometimes the enemy ships won't drop their bombs until they get further down the screen and closer to you. If you let them get in this position, you'll have a heck of a time trying to ditch them.

Stay at the bottom of the screen unless you have to move. This will give you more room to get away from enemy ships and the bombs they throw.

Several kinds of enemy ships fill the air. One is the Rotomech. These pesky ships rotate and come at you from different angles in a curve formation. Tempting as it may be, don't move around too much when the Rotomechs come at you. Find a place on the screen where you can hit one. Then, stay there. After you destroy the first few, move a little to the side to get the rest of them in your sights. These guys are easy to handle, but in the later stages, don't let them get too close to you. If they do, you'll have a few bombs with your name on them.

The Protodroids are almost as fun as the Rotomechs. They're famous for moving across the screen and bombing you. Two techniques work on these guys. The first is to just move along with them and take your shots. The second is to stay just outside their bomb range. Move into range to shoot, then scurry back again. They're history!

If you think you're out of trouble, you're wrong. The Harriers are about to harry you all over the screen. At first, they're a piece of cake. They come straight down the screen, and you can blast 'em, nice and easy. Once they get to the bottom of the screen, though, they move sideways and ram you from the side. And, that's not all. They cooperate. If you're not all the way to the bottom when one of them gets to the bottom, the others will try to ram you.

Shoot Pinchers early; blow them away before they have a chance to release their bombs.

Watch out for Arrowheads—they'll suddenly speed up. If you can shoot them early, do it. Otherwise, just let them pass. Keep an eye on them, and dodge their fire.

And there's more. Still to come are Skimbots and Macks. Both drive on the roads in Stage 3. Be careful of the laser beam on the Macks. If you're on a low power level, they'll take more than one shot at you. Zigzags are a kick. They move side to side in a jerky, annoying motion. The best way to deal with them is not to copy their movement. Just stay in one place, intercept their path, and blast them.

One of the toughest ships to destroy is the Terra Cannon, especially when they all get together and block the road in Stage 3. The best way to deal with these nasty road blockers is to continue shooting at them on one side of the road. Then, you'll be able to pass on that side without having to shoot all of them down.

In later stages (4 and above), the ships get more powerful. The Vexor shoots three bombs at the same time and makes it very difficult indeed to find a place to go. The War Hawk and Miditron have laser beams which make it a lot more difficult to avoid bombs. The most fearsome of all is the Blazer which requires the most powerful turbo missiles to kill.

So far it's been all bad news. Your glimmer of hope is in the power pod. These fellows always come straight down the middle of the screen. Shoot one, and it turns into a power-up item. The first time you run over one, your firepower will increase from one shooter to two. Every two you get after that increases your firepower from single shot, to double shot, to triple shot, and finally (the ultimate power) turbo missiles. Beware. Each time you get blown away, you will go down one firepower level. Most important of all is to not get careless when reaching for the power pods. You may run right into enemy fire. Not only do you lose the increased power, but you go down one level because you just got blown away. In the same vein, don't get so focused on shooting the attacking ships that you miss the power-up items.

Tec's Tips

I like to focus on the big old bosses at the end of each stage. Each of the bosses behaves differently and requires several shots to kill. For example, the Stage 1 boss, Epikhan, moves left and right, firing bombs in a particular pattern that limits the number of places you can hide. The Stage 2 boss, Destructor, fires bubble bombs that you can shoot to avoid getting bombed. Beware when the boss moves down right on top of you. Hide in the corner until he goes back up, then start shooting.

The bosses keep getting trickier and trickier as you go. For example, the Stage 3 boss, Ultra Crusher, has laser beams that are tougher to get away from. Ultra Crusher's lasers shoot across at the bottom so you can't hide in the corner any more. The later stage bosses are made of several parts; you have to kill each part individually.

Keep two important points in mind when fighting stage bosses. First, avoid getting blown away right before the stage ends. That reduces your firepower—you'll have to hit the boss many more times to kill him. Second, don't concentrate on every shot hitting the boss. Pay more attention to dodging his bombs. If you stay away from his bombs, you'll eventually kill the bad, old boss—it just may take a little longer.

Other Pointers

- Always shoot your enemy before the enemy has time to shoot back.
- Know when to keep moving.
- Shoot power pods to get the power-up items for more firepower.

■ Be defensive. Sometimes the best strategy is to run and avoid the fight.

Manufacturer Information

Company: Nintendo of America Inc.
Address: P.O. Box 957
Redmond, Washington
98073-0957
Game Play Counselors: 206-885-7529 (This is a regular toll charge telephone call.)
Typical Price: $24.99

Space Invaders

Description

Oh no! It's the return of *Space Invaders*. Actually, "Oh, yes!" is a better statement. *Space Invaders* is THE classic arcade hit. Now you can wow the competition on Game Boy just the way you did in the public video arcade.

Boom, boom, boom. They're after you. Stop the marching hordes of space aliens before they get you. Level after level, wave after wave, you continue to be vulnerable. But, accurate firing and quick defensive moves keep you alive to continue on.

Warning: Don't take this game to the office or to school. It can get you in trouble in more ways than one. Either you'll never put the game down or you'll never see your Game Boy again. Seems like everyone knows how to play this game.

Let's Play

Use the following buttons to control your ship and zap the enemy:

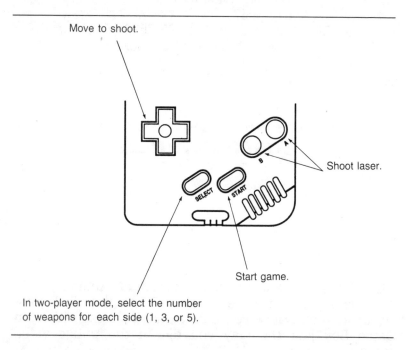

Move to shoot.

Shoot laser.

Start game.

In two-player mode, select the number of weapons for each side (1, 3, or 5).

The guys with legs (officially known as Invaders 1st Class) are worth 10 points. The guys with antennae (Invaders 2nd Class) are worth 20 points. The funny looking coneheads (Invaders 3rd Class) are worth 30 points. For really big points, the UFO flying saucers that occasionally run across the top of the screen are worth a bundle.

If you play with two people, you need two Game Boy systems, a *Space Invaders* cartridge in each, and a Video Link. When you play in tandem, you get to pick the number of weapons each player gets. You may have 1, 2, or 3 weapons per side.

There are some other differences when you play in twos. A real kick is the ability to control the flying saucer. You can also send bad news to your friend. Just shoot up a row or column of five invaders, and they teleport to your buddy's screen.

When two people play, you can win either by being the first to get through five rounds of swarming invaders or by wasting your pal's flying saucers. You can also win in a passive sort of way by defending yourself long enough that the invader's press eats up your friend at the bottom of the screen.

Strategies

Hi's Hints

The whole family plays this one. It's easy to learn and easy to play. But it's also really addictive. I think it owes its popularity to the fact that it's a simple concept and simple game. You get success right away, but there's always the desire to improve your score. The marching sound does something to get you going too.

My approach is to scoot over to the right of each screen and start there. I try to stay in front of the marching invaders because I find that when I'm behind them, I'm more likely to run into a laser and get fried.

I like to get a good start on wiping out a whole column at a time. Hit the first guy on the right side, then keep firing. These guys are so dumb they just keep marching in your line of fire. If you're set up just right, you can get the column with a few easy shots. Get in the right position, and you'll be able to do this over and over again, cleaning up bunches of guys quickly.

The barrier on the right of the screen is a good place to hide—you'll be less likely to get wiped out than if you use the ones on the left.

If you like the barriers, try this: Shoot a hole through the barrier, then sit behind it and shoot through the hole at the enemies. It takes some time to make the hole, and eventually your barrier gets destroyed, but it's fun while it lasts.

When the guys get to the bottom of the screen, they start moving faster. This is when I switch to shooting rows just to pull through. You have to kill those invaders who are closest to you to survive. This is your only defense. First they'll wipe out your barriers, then they'll ram you to your death.

If you really start sweating, press the Start button to pause. You can still see an image of the screen to assess how much trouble you're in and what your strategy will be. When you press Start again, be ready to go like the devil.

Tec's Tips

I primarily pay a lot of attention to my shooting. I find that randomly shooting doesn't work that well. You can't just hold down a button and get rapid fire. Plus, once you shoot, there is some reload time before you can shoot again. Your finger can definitely go faster than the game can fire off. Because of these limitations, you need to get the finger/button timing down to make the most of every split second. And, you need to make the most of each shot. One poorly placed shot may keep you from blasting off a good, clean shot when you really need to.

Because the guys are marching at you, this is both a game of skill and of time. The closer they get, the faster they go. Do whatever you can to kill more guys fast.

Don't panic when they shoot at you. Often, their aim is bad (after all, they're just blasting away haphazardly). You may be able to tap the directional button to slide just a little to one side or another and avoid the laser.

You can destroy the enemy's shots with your own, but it won't always work. As a shot skims over your head, you'll find yourself saying "I know I got that one!" Generally though, your shots will stop theirs.

I only go for the spaceship and the big bonus if the invaders are a safe distance away and I have a decent shot. If I have invaders breathing down my neck, chasing the spaceship across the screen is a waste of precious time.

Once you play a while, you'll get a sense of when the spaceship is coming across. You'll develop a pattern for handling each screen, including improving your point game.

The single player game offers fifty levels. As you progress, the invaders get faster and the points get higher. You can amuse yourself for a long time before you get up there.

Other Pointers

- Random shooting can waste more time than invaders. Plan your shots.

- Anticipate where the invader will be when your shot reaches him.

- Don't run into the lasers. Avoid them by running, or deflect them with your own fire.

- Get a sense of how long it takes a laser to reach the spaceship. You have to time the shot just right for the spaceship to meet with your blaster.

- When you wipe out a column, go for a column on the edges. The invaders only move down when they hit an edge, so you'll buy yourself some precious time.

103

Manufacturer Information

Company: Taito
Address: 267 West Esplanade
North Vancouver, B.C., Canada
V7M1A5
Technical Support: 604-984-3040 (This is a regular
toll charge telephone call.)
Typical Price: $24.95

Super Mario Land

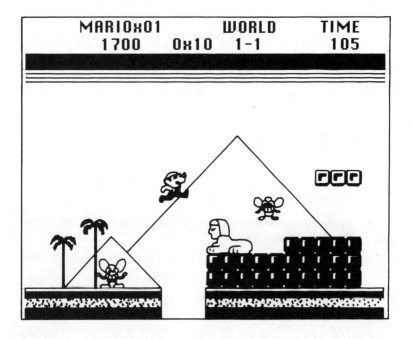

Description

That's right, you can now take the Mario brothers on the road with *Super Mario Land*. In this caper, the space freak Tatanga has taken over serene Sarasaland and is out to marry dear Princess Daisy. Don't let him do it. This is not someone you'd want marrying your daughter, Princess Daisy, or any other fair maiden for that matter. To stop Tatanga, you must defeat him.

Let's Play

Use the following controls to move Mario around the screen and shoot missiles and torpedoes:

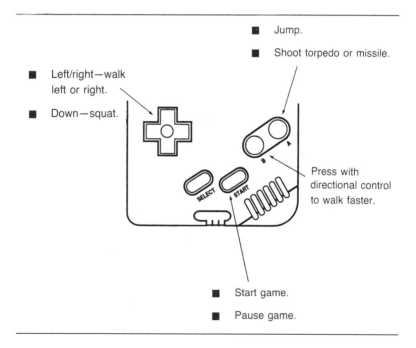

■ Jump.

■ Shoot torpedo or missile.

■ Left/right—walk left or right.

■ Down—squat.

Press with directional control to walk faster.

■ Start game.

■ Pause game.

The screen shows how many Marios are left, your score, the number of coins you have, the World/Area you're in, and the time remaining. There are three areas in each of the following four worlds:

Birabuto

Muda

Easton

Chai

Destroy the boss at the end of the world, then step on the switch in front of the gate to move to the next world. Each area has an upper and lower entrance. The top one lets you play a bonus game; just press the B button.

Go for 1-UP hearts, extra Marios, coins (100 for an extra Mario), or mystery blocks for a surprise. Flowers, stars, and super mushrooms make Mario power up. The super mushroom creates a Super Mario. Add a flower for Superball Mario. A star makes Mario invincible.

Strategies

Hi's Hints

If you are playing *Super Mario Land* for the first time, I recommend that you take your time and practice using the controls. You should remember that when you're jumping with the A button, you must keep the button pressed to get the most height and distance. Remember, also, that when you're in the air you can still control Mario's movement. You can kill most of the enemies, except for the Boss of each world by jumping on them.

Remember that for each one hundred coins you collect, you receive an extra Mario life; for each one hundred thousand points you collect, you get another game. It's a good idea to take your time and collect all of the coins and kill all of the enemy characters. Don't just rush through each world.

Since the big deal in this game is to find hidden helps and kill bad guys, Tec and I decided to divide up our comments by world. So here's what I've found in World 1.

In World 1, Area 1, the third pipe leads to a hidden treasure room. Jump on top of the pipe and push down on the bottom of the directional control. Look for the 1-UP. It's hidden in the fourth break-away block in the group of six. Go on to Area 2 and you'll find a 1-UP heart in an invisible block near the bottom above a platform. Another 1-UP heart is in the third block in the second group of five blocks.

As soon as you get to Area 3 in World 1, look for the elevator along the left wall. Jump up along the left wall and bump your head on the invisible block. Jump on top of the elevator using the run button—this lifts you to the top of the screen. There, you can collect 28 coins. Don't forget to go down the first pipe you come to after you jump down from the top of the screen. This will lead you to yet another hidden room with a bunch of coins. An elevator is located in this room with a Gao inside. (Look for it in the invisible block just above the fourth block in the group of five.) Go down the pipe at the top of the screen, and collect the coins. In this room there's a 1-UP heart in the highest block on the right side.

Okay, assuming you made it through the areas, you come smack up against King Totomesu. The easiest way to get this guy is to be a Superball Mario and throw five superballs to kill the dude. Use expert timing and jump over him. He'll exhibit some bad behavior, such as jumping and spewing fire at you. Don't be afraid. Just run toward him, jump over him, and keep pelting him with fireballs.

World 2 is full of treasure, platforms, and pipes. You can build on the techniques you learned in World 1. In

Area 1, there is an invisible block at the beginning just under the first high platform with three coins. Take a look around and you'll find two hidden treasure rooms. (Check every pipe.) In one of the treasure rooms, there's an invisible block along the left wall. You can find it without too much trouble.

In World 2, Area 2, you'll find an invisible platform along the bottom of the screen that will allow you to "take the low road." However, this only works if you aren't Super Mario. To get to this platform, you must make a giant "leap of faith" to the right just under the vertical row of coins. Don't forget the hidden treasure room in this area.

Finally, you come to Area 3 in World 2. You are now Marine Pop, and you have to torpedo as many blocks and characters as you can. Here it is best to avoid hitting Gunions. If you do, they split in two and attack. They can give you some trouble. Power-up items abound in the break-away blocks, so be sure to hit them all. Since this is a scrolling screen, make sure you have a clear passage in front of you. (Remember that Torion always travel in groups of three.)

At the end of World 2, you get to fuss with Dragon-zamasu and Tamao. Move around the room and fire your torpedoes while you avoid the spits of fire and Tamao. It's easier than you might think.

That's about all I can tell you for these Worlds. Take over, Tec!

 ## Tec's Tips

Oh yeah. Stick me with the harder worlds, Hi. I guess it's my superior ability, huh?

Okay. In World 3, Area 1, watch out for the Batadons. As they fly around. They'll bounce down and crush Mario. It's tricky to kill them. Also, beware of the Tokotoko—they're fast. In this area, you must ride the Ganchan rocks. Don't worry, it's easier than it sounds. Watch out for the spikes along the bottom of the screen. Look for two hidden treasure rooms in this area.

In World 3, Area 2 there's an invisible block just to the right and above the top row of three blocks. This will allow you to jump to the top of the screen to collect coins and avoid the Suu. Don't miss the elevator in the invisible block above the third block in the second group of five. Using this, you can get to the pipe and coins at the top of the screen. There are several treasure rooms in this area.

In Area 3, a Ganchan rock may suddenly appear and try to squish you. Don't miss the hidden treasure room in the pipe that's in midair and the many hidden objects in the blocks.

When you get to the end of World 3, the not so friendly Hiyoihoi shows its ugly face. If you are a Superball Mario, you can hit it with ten superballs. I think the easiest way to slip by the Hiyoihoi is to just run through it. The down side is that you will be reduced to a regular Mario. The up side is that you will at least complete the world.

Now you are in the final world, World 4. In Area 1, don't miss the treasure room accessible through the first pipe to the left as the screen appears. As you go down the pipe, keep your thumb on the right side of the control pad. This is really the only way to collect any coins in this room. Your total success in this area depends on how good you are at stunning the Pionpi. In this area, you must be aware that the upside-down Pakkun do not hide when Mario is nearby.

Toward the middle of World 4, Area 2, you'll notice a row of break-away blocks at the top of the screen. If you can bump the first block, a star will pop out. Look for an invisible block along the left side of the wall near the vertically moving platform. If you find it, you can get a 1-UP heart. This can be a really tough area. Take your time.

In World 4, Area 3, Mario is Sky Pop. When you find items hidden in the blocks, you must catch them; otherwise, they just fall off the screen.

The Biokinton and the Tatanga are the dreaded enemies at the end of World 4. All you have to do to kill the

Biokinton is to stay in front of him and make sure you hit
everything he fires at you. If he gets too close, you must
move up or down and wait until he backs up. To kill Tatanga, maintain a position between the rockets he fires at
you. As you're maintaining this position, fire at regular
intervals. It may take a while, but you can do it.

Other Pointers

- As you are going through each world, make sure
  to break away all the blocks you can. Don't miss
  anything. Gain as many points as possible.

- Remember to take your time with the bonus
  game. Keep in mind what you need from each
  bonus game. If you're just a regular Mario,
  consider going for the flower.

- As a rule of thumb, it helps at the end of the
  worlds to be Superball Mario. He usually has the
  most luck against the bosses.

- Run when you jump, and old Mario will jump
  higher.

- Press the B button with the directional control to
  run right across the little openings in the ground.

- Pick a super flower to throw a superball.

- You have to be in the shooting area to fire a
  torpedo or missile.

Manufacturer Information

Company: Nintendo of America Inc.
Address: P.O. Box 957
         Redmond, Washington
         98073-0957

Game Play Counselors: 206-885-7529 (This is a
regular toll charge telephone call.)
Typical Price: $19.99

Tennis

Description

Game Boy *Tennis* is tennis the way you like it. Serve, lob,
volley, and smash your way to a win. If you're a beginner, start at a low skill level and move on to play with
greater expertise as you learn. Much love.

111

Let's Play

Use the following controls to serve, move your player, and smash your way to victory:

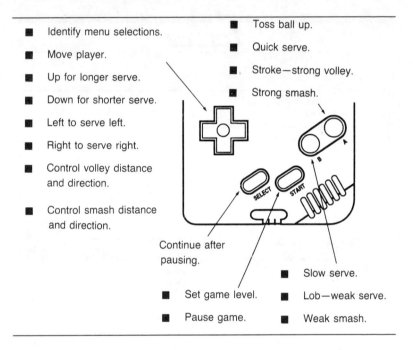

- Identify menu selections.
- Move player.
- Up for longer serve.
- Down for shorter serve.
- Left to serve left.
- Right to serve right.
- Control volley distance and direction.
- Control smash distance and direction.

- Toss ball up.
- Quick serve.
- Stroke—strong volley.
- Strong smash.

Continue after pausing.

- Set game level.
- Pause game.

- Slow serve.
- Lob—weak serve.
- Weak smash.

You can play *Tennis* with one or two players, and choose any of four levels of play. (Level 1 is the easiest.)

During the game, you may see the Score display and the display for actual game play. Additional screens are available in this order if you press the Select button during Pause:

Point display

Set game display

Count display

Match/level display

Strategies

Hi's Hints

Tennis is a very challenging game. It's set up like the old *Pong* game, except in *Tennis* you have to swing at the ball. There's no time limit, and the game is scored just like a real tennis match. Nintendo's own Mario plays the part of the umpire or line judge—any call he makes is final. There may be some questionable calls, but there can be no dispute as to whether the ball was in bounds or out.

If you're just getting started, begin at Level 1. Each time you go up a level, the speed of play increases and, of course, the difficulty increases. If you can beat the computer at Level 1, it will offer you a rematch at Level 2. This happens for the upper levels as well. The upper levels may seem a little fast at first, but after you get a little practice under your belt, you'll become a formidable opponent for the computer. After playing for a short time, you'll figure out how to place your shot wherever you want it, but even with that skill, it will take awhile before you can beat the computer at Level 2.

The only skills involved in *Tennis* have to do with following the ball and being able to hit the ball correctly. As the ball moves across the court, you'll see a tiny gray dot directly below it at all times. This is the ball's shadow. Use the shadow to keep track of where the ball is and how high off the ground it is.

Use the directional control for two things—to move your player around the court and to place your shots in the opposite court. For example, if you want to hit the ball into the upper right corner of the court, press the upper right part of the directional control. Use the bottom half of the directional control to hit a drop shot. Be careful with the drop shot. If you're too far from the net, you'll end up hitting the ball right into it. Work on getting a feel for how far you are from the net.

The game gives you two options for serving—the normal serve and the "quick serve". To perform a normal serve, just toss the ball up, and hit it on the way down. To hit a quick serve, hit the ball right after you toss it.

Tec's Tips

Once you get the basics down pat, you'll want to concentrate on playing well. I've got a few pointers to get you playing well, fast.

My big tip is how to "cheat" the computer. In Level 3, you can ace the computer. You need to serve from the right side of the court, and you need to hit a quick serve. As you're hitting the serve, keep pressing the left side of the directional control. The ball will shoot over to the extreme left side of the computer's court just out of its reach.

When the computer or the other player runs up to the net, you have one of two choices. You can lob it over his head with the hope that it will bounce too high for him to return, or you can hit a drop shot with the hope it will be too low for him to return. If you're good at the drop shot, it's a great shot to use.

You can use the quick serve to catch the other player off guard. It doesn't work against the computer player, however; the computer always pays attention. To beat the computer, you need to know how it operates. Many times, the computer is slow to move after it returns a serve. For example, if you serve to the extreme right or left, the computer will just stand there after it returns the ball. Take advantage of this lull. Return his return to the opposite side of his court so he can't get to it. This works well in the first two levels.

The lob shot is only good if the opponent is at the net or you want to slow down the play a bit. The lob gives your opponent the opportunity to smash the ball over the net and score. When you are playing in the upper levels, you'd better know when to hit the lob. If the computer player is at the net and you whack the ball, the computer will smash it even harder. In such a case, the lob might be best.

Other Pointers

- Watch out, it's possible to get beaned by the ball if you're standing in line and you don't swing in time.

- The worst thing to do is hit the ball right back to the computer or the other player. Keep the other player on the run so she can't place her shots.

Manufacturer Information

Company: Nintendo of America Inc.
Address: P.O. Box 957
Redmond, Washington
98073-0957
Game Play Counselors: 206-885-7529 (This is a
regular toll charge telephone call.)
Typical Price: $19.99

Tetris

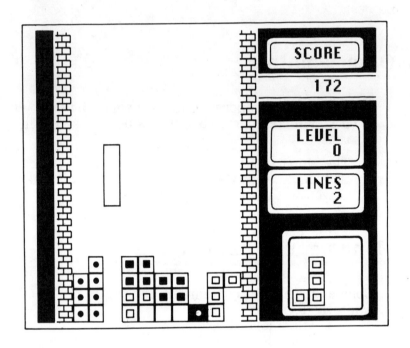

Description

On the surface, *Tetris* seems like a boring game. Blocks fall from the screen, and you have to piece them together at the bottom to complete lines of blocks. But when you start playing, you won't be able to put it down. As you get better and faster, the blocks fall faster and faster, until it looks as though it's raining blocks.

Tetris requires a combination of visual quickness, spatial skill, and some very quick fingers. Old and young alike will find plenty of challenge in this apparently simple game. A real expert can reveal the shooting space-ships and Russian dancers. Good luck, comrade!

Let's Play

Use the following buttons to control the falling blocks:

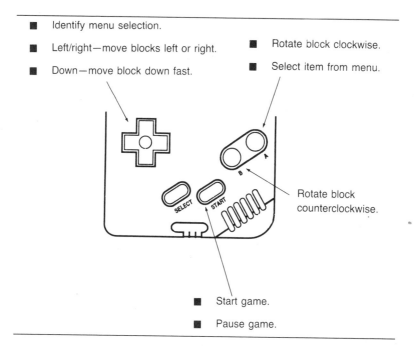

- Identify menu selection.
- Left/right—move blocks left or right.
- Down—move block down fast.
- Rotate block clockwise.
- Select item from menu.
- Rotate block counterclockwise.
- Start game.
- Pause game.

As I said, the game is simple. Blocks of seven different shapes fall from the sky. Your goal is to position each block, as it is falling, so it fits together with the other blocks at the bottom of the screen. Complete one line of blocks, and the line disappears, giving you points. Once the blocks pile up to the top, you're dead.

You may choose the level of difficulty and music through menu screens. These three games are available:

Game A—complete as many lines as you can. The level controls the speed of the falling blocks.

Game B—complete 25 lines for your total score. The level controls the speed of the blocks. The height controls the height of the beginning block pile. (You have to work around a preexisting pile.)

Two-player—send extra lines of blocks to your pal. Complete 2 lines at once and your partner gets 1 line. Do 3 lines, and he or she gets 2 lines. Complete a Tetris (4 lines), and your pal gets all 4 lines. Some friend you are!

Strategies

Hi's Hints

When you first get going with *Tetris*, play the B type game. This game is sudden death—when the blocks reach the top of the screen, the game is over. The object here is to build 25 lines of blocks before the stack of blocks reaches the ceiling. It can get pretty interesting at the end. You might have one or two lines to complete, and the stack may be getting dangerously close to the ceiling. Don't panic. No matter how high the stack, if you get those 25 lines, you win.

Once you're an expert, you can play with the most interesting and challenging feature of the B game: height. The game normally begins with a height of 0 (zero); that is, no blocks on screen. You can change this setting to make the game more challenging. Select a height of 1 through 5, and the screen will start you off with a preexisting stack of blocks. You need to figure out how to work with that stack to win the game.

In the B game, you can fill in the gaps as you see them, but it's more important to complete some lines and get them off the screen. For example, if you get the straight, 1x4 piece, lay it on its side to fill in a line rather than standing it on end to fill a 1-block gap. This will give you a complete line sooner. Use the Z-, T-, or L-shaped pieces to fill in the small gaps.

Once you get the hang of the game, try out the A type game. In this game, you keep going until you get to the top of the screen. The more you score, the faster the pieces fall. Looks like a hail storm!

The best strategy in the A game is to try to build high and to the sides. Drop blocks in the middle to complete lines and keep your stack of blocks as low as possible. Because the pieces fall from the top of the screen, having a high stack in the middle forces you to quickly move pieces to the side without much time to consider the best use for the piece.

In the higher levels, when the pieces fall faster, it is downright critical to have a low stack. You need the extra time to decide what to do with the falling pieces.

The single, most important skill to master in this game is the ability to combine blocks in various ways for the best results. Always fill in the most difficult gaps first. For example, if you have a gap 3 blocks tall and 1 block wide, the only piece to fill the gap is the 1x4 piece. If that piece comes at you, use it to fill the gap instead of putting it somewhere else.

It is also important to know how pieces can be combined to form other shapes. For example, if you have the same color Z-shape piece, you can stack them on end (one on another) to build straight up. Or, if you have the same color L-shaped pieces, you can put two of them together to build a 2x4 rectangle. These more regular shapes are easier to work around.

Avoid leaving a hole in the middle of a stack of blocks. If you do, you must complete the lines above the hole first. Those lines will then disappear, leaving the hole open. If you do leave a hole, don't panic. Just try to keep from stacking blocks any higher. Clear those lines.

Sometimes it is impossible to make the falling piece fit perfectly in place. For example, if a Z shape is the first one to drop, you're stuck. When the pieces just don't fit, make sure the hole you leave will be accessible from the side. You can slide a piece into the hole from the side, but you have to be quick. Position the piece just right. When it drops down next to the hole, press the left or right side of the directional control to slide it into place. If you're too slow, the piece will lock into place before you can slide it.

Tec's Tips

You can rotate pieces in either of two ways. Use the A button to rotate counterclockwise. Use the B button to rotate clockwise. Practice these moves until you don't have to think about them. The higher levels won't give you time to think. (Don't worry about the A or B button for pieces that are symmetrical. It doesn't matter which direction you rotate those guys.)

The "next piece" feature is really helpful. It shows you which piece will fall next. Use it to make better decisions. For example, if there's a gap on the side that's getting high, use one of the L-shaped pieces in place of the 1x4 to give yourself more room. If the next piece is a 1x4, you may want to put the L-shaped piece somewhere else and use the 1x4 to fill the long gap.

Another feature of the game lets you control the speed of the falling pieces to rack up more points. Hold down the down arrow, and the pieces fall faster. The higher you drop the piece from, the faster it drops, and the more points you get. That is, as long as the piece falls in just the right spot. Rotate the piece at the very top of the screen. Get it in just the right position. Then, press the down arrow, fast!

At the higher levels, you might want to let the pieces fall by themselves. Use the extra time to position the pieces more effectively and clear more lines. The more lines you can complete with a single piece, the more points you get. Get 2 lines at the same time, and you get

2.5 times the points you'd get for a single line. You get 7.5 times for 3. Complete a Tetris, and you get a whopping 30 times the points! That's the absolute best way to rack up points.

Go for a Tetris. Purposefully build your blocks leaving a gap that's one block wide and four high. Then, when you get the 1x4 piece, slide it in, nice and easy.

Other Pointers

- Get to 100,000 points in the A game, and a big rocket takes off.

- In the B game, when you successfully complete 25 lines at each height on Level 9, you'll see Russian dancers. The dancers increase up to Height 4, where the screen is full of dancers jumping with joy. Feel free to jump up and down with them—you have just completed a difficult task.

- Complete Level 9, Height 5 in the B game and you'll see the space shuttle take off.

- Always keep your options open by filling in the most difficult gaps first. Think ahead by placing the next piece in your mind before it starts falling.

- For a game more difficult than Level 9 and Height 5, press down the directional button and press Start during the title screen. Then, go, go, go!

Manufacturer Information

Company: Nintendo of America Inc.
Address: P.O. Box 957
Redmond, Washington
98073-0957
Game Play Counselors: 206-885-7529 (This is a
regular toll charge telephone call.)
Typical Price: Free with purchase of Game Boy.

The Bugs Bunny Crazy Castle

Description

What's up, Doc? *The Bugs Bunny Crazy Castle*. And when you're in this game, you'll be wondering not only what's up, but what's down, around, and sideways. Daffy Duck, Sylvester, Wiley Coyote, and Yosemite Sam have kidnapped sweet Honey Bunny and hidden her somewhere in this 60 room castle of lunacy. You have to pick up carrots, avoid those scalawags, and make your way through corridors, dungeons, and mazes, in search of your Honey.

Let's Play

These buttons put you in control of the game, and in control of Bugs himself:

■ Move Bugs.

■ Identify password letters.

■ Identify menu selections.

Punch with boxing glove.

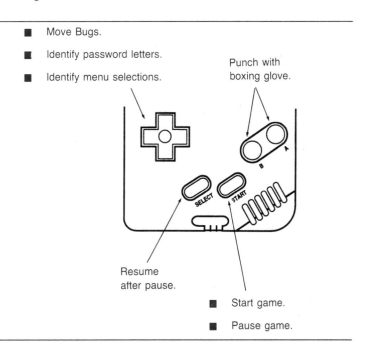

Resume after pause.

■ Start game.

■ Pause game.

123

You can begin the game in either of two ways. If you want to start at the beginning, select Game Start from the opening screen. If you want to start at a point later in the game, select Password, and then enter the password required to get you into the later room. If you enter a password, press Start to get to the level.

As you play, pick up all the carrots in a room to proceed to the next room. When you finish a room, you get a life, a password for the level, and you may choose Video to watch the level again. Keep an eye out for these goodies:

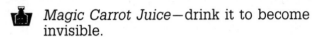 *Magic Carrot Juice*—drink it to become invisible.

Boxing Glove—to punch the bad guys.

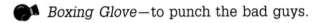 *Safe, Wooden Crate, Bucket, and Ten Ton Weight*—to push over (or on) a rascal.

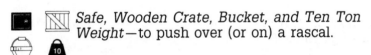 *No-Carrot Sign*—to play a tough level where you may gain three lives.

Be quick like a "wabbit" and you're sure to win.

Strategies

Hi's Hints

This is an easy game, perfect for kids and adults alike. You start out with five (fairly generous) lives. You will come to only three types of rooms:

Mazes of stairways

Mazes of pipes

Mazes of doors

The rooms get more difficult as you proceed, but after each room, you earn a life. As you go, you'll find the rooms have more bad guys and require more complex moves to get through. I think it's a super game.

At the end of every level is a password. You can use the password to reenter that level. For example, you can jump in a third of the way through at Stage 20 with the code ZTPZ. You can get in two thirds of the way through (Stage 40) with TX9W. Get all the way to the final stage with YTKX. Write down the codes for the levels you might want to reenter. When you're entering the codes, just hold down the keys, and the game will scroll through the letters—you don't have to tap your way through.

If you need to take a break, to get an ice cold coke or a bag of chips, you can't just lay the game down—those "wascally" critters will come and git you. Instead, use the Start button to pause.

The whole strategy of this game is to run away from the bad guys unless, of course, you have a secret power or you can push something over on them. I move cautiously through the game trying to stay behind things I can push or drop on their little heads.

The object of each level is to get all the carrots. If you get all of them, you wave your arms and move to the next level (and get the password on the way). You'll also see "1 up." That means that you've just picked up a free Bugs Bunny life on your way to the next level.

When you get to a new level, don't just start picking up carrots. Run around and get a feel for the lay-out. Take note of any corners where you might get trapped. Look for boxing gloves and carrot juice. On each level, try to figure out a strategy or pattern. You might benefit by getting the objects in a certain order.

You get 100 points for each carrot and 1000 points for each bad guy that you bump off. You can knock off a bad guy in either of two ways. Drop an object on his head or push it over on him; the second way is a little easier.

There's a no-carrot sign on some of the levels. When you run into it, you go to a special level. If you win the level, you get three lives. The special level is difficult to beat. It's a good idea to avoid the level unless you're a super expert or are almost out of lives anyway.

Climbing stairs takes a little bit of practice. As you're approaching the stairs, press up a little on the directional control. This will move you diagonally up the stairs. This way, you won't have to stop at the bottom of the stairs.

You don't always have to use the stairs or elevators to proceed. It may be easier to just hop off the stairs or off a ledge. Plan your hop for the best advantage.

Tec's Tips

Each rascal moves in a particular pattern on a level. Watch each character. Figure out the pattern, and get the timing down. Move to the right position, and you can punch or push an object over at just the right moment—the guy won't know what hit him.

Unlike some games, in this game the bad guys don't have a clue about where you are early in the game. Just like you, they're wandering around, getting a feel for the turf. If you can make a good evasive move, they aren't necessarily going to follow right after you. Later in the game, they do become aware of your whereabouts and follow you. Hide out below them on the stairs under the elevator and fake them out. Get them to go in one direction, then run the opposite way. Get in position to beat them.

Be particularly careful about getting near the edge of the screen. This is especially true at the higher levels. When you get to the edge, you don't have many options. You can't fake them out, and there's nowhere to run. The bad guys will run over and bite you—you're history.

When you die, you start out in the level where you died, but you don't pick up where you left off. You have to get all of the goodies again.

Each level contains two boxing gloves. It's a good idea to pick up a boxing glove early on. A boxing glove gives you a lot of options for defense, and you can use it at any time. When you use it, you have to be aiming in the direction you want to punch.

As the levels get more advanced, you cannot squander your opportunity to push an object over on the rascals. Often there are just barely enough boxing gloves, safes, wooden crates, buckets, and ten ton weights to nail all the rascals on the level. You can avoid them, but it's easier to kill them (if you have the resources).

Other Pointers

- If you've died on a level, before you go back in, use the Video option. This will show you a computerized replay of everything you did. The replay can reveal some important patterns, as well as your mistakes. You can also see where the goodies are.

- Patience is a virtue. When you're on a new level, take your time and scout out the bad guys. They won't run right over, so take some time to look and plan.

- Being invisible by drinking carrot juice is GREAT. Not only are you invincible, but you can kill all the bad guys. You don't get points for killing them, but they're out of the picture, and you can go about your business of carrot hunting. Pick your invisible time and wipe out a bunch of guys. It doesn't last long, so hurry.

Manufacturer Information

Company: Seika Corporation, USA
Address: 20000 Mariner Avenue, Suite 100
        Torrance, CA
        90503

Telephone: 1-800-462-5040
Typical Price: $24.00

The Castlevania Adventure

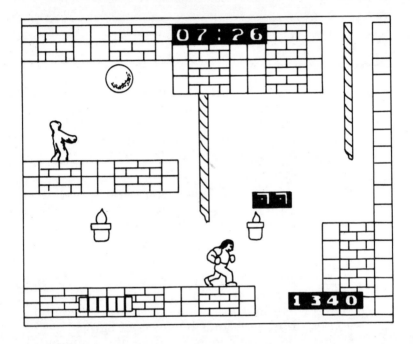

Description

The evil Count Dracula is at it again, attacking every ten-
der neck he can sink his teeth into. Evade or kill Count
Dracula's bad guys or you'll be just another meal for his
bloodthirsty crew. Your major weapons are the mighty

whip and the fierce fireball. Luck? It won't get you by. This is a game of timing and skill.

Let's Play

Use the following buttons to evade the Count and destroy his minions:

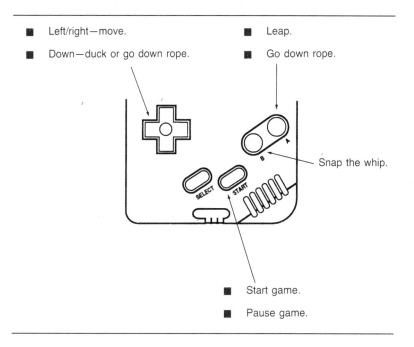

■ Left/right—move.

■ Down—duck or go down rope.

■ Leap.

■ Go down rope.

— Snap the whip.

■ Start game.

■ Pause game.

With only three lives, you'll need pass through four levels of ugliness in this adventure. Each level has it's own special creep guarding the end. As you proceed through the levels, you can whip candles to light them and to get the following items:

 A heart to give you more life.

 A flashing heart for a full, new life line.

A 1-UP for an extra life.

 A gold cross to be invincible for a while.

 A crystal to boost your whipping power. (One gives you a longer, stronger whip. Two give you fireballs. There is no benefit for more than two while you have fireball power.)

 A flashing crystal to call for the Primary Evil in the level.

 A coin for points.

To get an additional life, go for 10,000 points. At every 20,000, you'll get another life. Your life line appears at the bottom of the screen along with the points you've accumulated. At the top of the screen is the time limit. Balance your point-taking with your time—in this game, every millisecond counts.

Strategies

 ### Hi's Hints

The Castlevania Adventure is a pure adventure. You take a journey and pick up objects on the way. Evil guys lurk everywhere. If you know the secret to getting around them, you'll succeed. If not, watch your neck!

One of the most important elements of this game consists of finding the objects you need to defeat each Primary Evil. On each of the four levels there's a hidden room which contains these objects. Pick up the objects, and you'll have an easier time defeating the main boss at the end of the level. Here's what I've found.

In Level 1, you'll climb some ropes. As you climb the fifth rope (which should be on the right side), you'll find yourself in a screen with an Under Mole crawling toward you. Keep going up the rope even though it appears that you'll climb through a brick. When you do, the screen changes to the next room, and you can pick up a coin, a crystal, a 1-UP, and a flashing heart.

In Level 2, several routes will get you to the hidden screen. The passage to the hidden screen is just a few screens after the long bridge. Look for the screen with four large steps going down from left to right. Stand at the bottom step facing left. When a Big Eye falls to the third step, whip it. The explosion will blow away the top of the step. Scramble into the hole, if it's big enough. If the hole is too small, you'll have to nail another Big Eye over the hole. All the Big Eye destruction is well worth it, since you'll find the coins, a crystal, a 1-UP, and a flashing heart.

On to Level 3. Toward the end of this level, you'll come to a screen filled with bricks. Look for the rope on the left. Try climbing two thirds of the way up the rope then jump off to the right. Continue to press the right side of the control pad, and you'll end up at the bottom of a hidden screen. In here, you'll find three useful items. You'll need them all for the nasty ascent.

If you've been doing a bang-up job getting hidden objects and using them to your advantage, you'll make it to Level 4. You can get to this hidden screen through the high-ceiling room with a rope on each side and a Zeldo in the middle. After you kill the Zeldo, climb two thirds of the way up the rope to the left. Land on an invisible platform. Position yourself just under the middle of the ceiling, jump up, and climb through an invisible hole. The next room contains three items. You'll need these for your final quest to defeat Count Dracula.

Happy hunting!

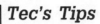 ***Tec's Tips***

I've concentrated a lot on how to defeat the enemies. You have to know their weak spots and what objects are needed. Otherwise, you may try and try and get nowhere. For example, if the Big Eye is rolling to you, jump over it unless there's another one in close pursuit. If another one is coming, you have to press down on the control pad and devastate the Big Eye. If you don't press down on the control pad, you'll miss— the Big Eye is just too low for you to hit standing up. It's a whole lot easier to get it when it's falling down the steps.

The She Worm is a whole other challenge. You must be careful when attacking this creature. Sometimes when you kill the She Worm, it will curl into a ball and roll away. In some instances, it might bounce back at you, so watch out!

The Punaguchi is tricky to kill, because you have to watch out for the fireballs that it spews at you. Once you get up close, it takes at least two lashes of your whip depending on how powerful your whip is.

There are two different types of Death Bats. The small ones appear more often and are much less harmful than the larger ones. Go to the end of Level 3, and you'll see a large Death Bat; this is the primary evil. Frankly, the easiest way to do this guy in is to throw fireballs at it with your whip. If you can't seem to get that down, try this: Position yourself directly below the Death Bat and wait for it to swoop down. If you are positioned correctly, you should be able to whip it without being hit. You'll have to do it several times, so have patience and stamina.

The hideous Madman isn't as frightful to kill as it looks. These dudes like to drop down at you from the ceiling, so make sure you time your whips carefully.

Lucky for you, the Evil Armor guys only show up at the start of the fourth level. You don't know which guys will come to life, so beware.

There is more than one kind of Under Mole. The small ones appear throughout Level 1; the big, primary evil guys appear at the end of Level 2. To nail the large Under Moles, you have to whip them before they come out of their holes in the wall. If you can't reach their holes, it's best to station yourself so you can whip them as they hit the ground.

The Gobanz appear at the end of Level 1 and towards the end of Level 4. To trounce them, keep yourself at the right distance to whip them and avoid being hurt. You must have a long whip to do this. Fireballs don't do much good with these guys since they just bounce off the armor.

Zeldo appears toward the end of Level 2 and throughout the upper levels. When old Zeldo throws a boomerang claw at your head, duck to avoid it then jump when it comes back. If Zeldo crouches and throws one at your body, do the opposite. Creep in close enough to whip Zeldo at least twice.

Other Pointers

- To avoid the pursuing wall, don't waste your time trying to whip all the candles on the wall. If you do go for whipping all the candles, make sure you have plenty of time to get the job done.

- Before you pick up the flashing crystal at the end of each level, make sure you're in a good spot to take on a primary evil.

- The really nasty Count Dracula is difficult to defeat. The last screen of Level 4 has a bunch of small platforms positioned around the whole screen. When you pick up the flashing crystal, stay to the right of the platform, because Count Dracula will show up on your left. As he throws the little round objects in four different directions, jump over them and whip him at thesame time. When his position changes to the other side, all you have to do is move to the leftside of the same platform. This should take care of his first form. After that, he comes back in the form of a bat and sends forth four smaller bats to attack you. When this happens, jump up to the second platform (right or left) to jump and whip him when he goes by. This may be tricky because you may have to maneuver to other platforms to avoid being bitten.

- There is really no use for coins in this game unless you like a high score. Typically, they just slow you down.

- When jumping gaps in the bridge, you must time it perfectly; otherwise, it's hello death!

- You can't strike when you're scaling a rope.

- Jump Attack by holding down the A button and striking the B button.

Manufacturer Information

Company: Konami Inc.
Address: 900 Deerfield Parkway
         Buffalo Grove, Illinois
         60089-4510
Telephone: 708-215-5111 (This is a regular toll
         charge telephone call.)
Typical Price: $24.99

Quarth

Description

Quarth is a dripping *Tetris*. You need to fill in the ooze at the top of your screen and remove it in time. Otherwise, the ooze covers you and you're a goner.

Let's Play

These buttons put you in control of the game:

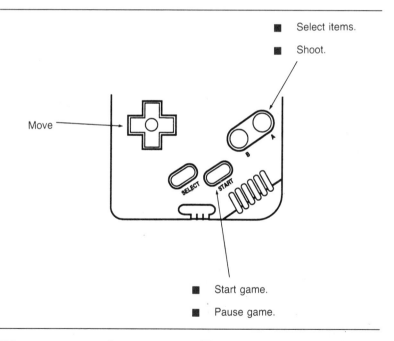

Move

■ Select items.

■ Shoot.

■ Start game.

■ Pause game.

When you start the game, you'll see three menus. One is for the level, one is for the stage in the level, and the third is for the icon you use at the bottom of the screen.

Use a combination of the Start button and A and B buttons to pick what you want.

In higher levels, the objects come down the screen more quickly. Experienced users may want to jump right in at higher levels for a real challenge. Patterns, numbers, and symbols appear at these higher levels.

Strategies

Hi's Hints

This is a good game for beginners. The materials don't move down the screen fast, and you can have a good deal of success at the start.

In *Quarth*, you're really not shooting to kill things; you're trying to get rid of the ooze. The ooze is made up of various patterns: some are L-shaped, some are T-shaped, etc. Your goal is to shoot at these various patterns to fill them in and turn them into rectangles. Form a rectangle, and that part of the ooze disappears.

If the L's are horizontal, fill in the missing part in the bottom of the area. Shoot and move, over and over, to fill it in. If the L is vertical, get underneath the missing part and shoot repeatedly to fill in the area.

When dealing with T-shaped objects, you must be careful not to shoot the middle part of the T. If you do, it makes the T longer, and you have more to deal with than the game originally gave you.

It's not unusual to see a long leg coming down the screen. If you see one of these long legs, go over and start shooting. If it's lying on the edge of the screen, it obviously has to be one of the long, skinny L's. If that's the case, when the top of the L appears, the shots will go toward completing the pattern.

Sometimes you'll see straight, horizontal bars. Put another line underneath that. Get near one end, shoot, and move to the next end.

Don't hang around and wait until all the rectangles disappear. Once you've fired enough shots to get rid of the rectangle, move on to the next one.

You can shoot more times than necessary to complete a rectangle. For example, if you need only four shots, you can shoot five or six times without getting messed up. But be careful—you can only overshoot the last row. For example, you'll see one pattern that looks like a square horseshoe. In order to get it, put three shots in, move over, and put three more shots in. You can overshoot the last three shots, and it won't matter, but if you overshoot the first three, you'll make the item longer and create more work for yourself. Overshooting doesn't help you all that much, but knowing that you can do it gives your trigger finger a little more freedom.

Tec's Tips

You don't always want to run back and forth to get the bottom material. The time it takes to move is substantial. Instead, wipe out some ooze and then move a short distance. Move smoothly only when you need to. Maximize your time shooting.

In more advanced levels, you'll complete a square that contains a hole in the middle. This will give you some bonus points.

I like to fill an area in an S pattern. I fill the top row then the next row and so on. This helps prevent me from putting too many shots in a column and adding to my troubles.

If you clean out a particularly large object on the screen, you can get a bonus. You may finish a figure then realize that it's part of a bigger rectangle that you didn't see. If the whole thing disappears, you get a bonus. Try this approach: If you're down to the last object on a screen, intentionally make it bigger by running the sides down. If it's large enough (20 or so small squares), you can fill it in for a bonus.

Other Pointers

- You can pick your icon from the menu at the bottom.

- If you think you're in trouble, you might not be. You could finish off some big area and receive a big bonus.

- Don't randomly shoot. It is more important to know where you are and shoot for a purpose. Random shots can get you in trouble.

- You can have a solid stream of shots in the air . . . just don't send too many.

- If you're trying to fill in a big object for big points, you can partially fill it in, work on filling some smaller objects in somewhere else, and then come back and complete the big object.

Manufacturer Information

Company: Konami Inc.
Address: 900 Deerfield Parkway
Buffalo Grove, IL
60089-4510
Telephone: 708-215-5111 (This is a regular toll charge telephone call.)
Typical Price: $19.99

Set Your Sights on Record-Breaking Scores with Games Books from Hayden

Mastering Nintendo Video Games

Judd Robbins and Joshua Robbins

The perfect companion for children and adults who want to master the most popular Nintendo games, with a strong emphasis on strategies as well as tips and techniques for improving the player's score. Covers more than 100 games and includes Super Mario Brothers 2, Double Dragon, Castlevania II: Simon's Quest, Bionic Commando, and Zelda II: The Adventures of Link.

ISBN 0-672-48464-1, $7.95 USA

Mastering Nintendo Video Games II

Judd Robbins and Joshua Robbins

New expanded coverage! Reveals shortcuts, booby traps, passwords, and strategies for more than 100 games. Features Mega Tips, hints, and secret weapons to set record-breaking scores. This updated version of the best-selling book covers these top games: Double Dragon II, Super Mario Brothers 3, Castlevania, and Tetris.

ISBN 0-672-48491-9, $9.95 USA

Winner's Guide to Sega Genesis

Kate Barnes

A comprehensive look at the best-selling games for Sega's Genesis Entertainment System. Packed with graphics, this book provides game-winning tips and strategies for serious gamers! Includes coverage of these hot games: Thunder Force II, Golden Axe, Alex Kidd, Tommy Lasorda Baseball, and many more!

ISBN 0-672-48489-7, $9.95 USA

Beyond the Nintendo Masters

Clayton Walnum and Andy Eddy

Written for Nintendo experts, this book provides clues and winning solutions to 17 of the hardest Nintendo games. *Beyond the Nintendo Masters* also offers detailed, advanced strategies and practice tips to set record-breaking scores early and often. Complete with game control illustrations!

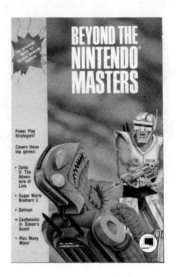

ISBN 0-672-48483-8, $9.95 USA